Research Methods

Creating New Knowledge

–DR. SAMWEL NYAGUCHA ORESI –

OCTOBER 2018

Published by New Generation Publishing in 2018

Copyright © Dr. Samwel Nyagucha Oresi 2014

First Edition

The author asserts the moral right under the Copyright, Designs and Patents Act 1988 to be identified as the author of this work.

All Rights reserved. No part of this publication may be reproduced, stored in a retrieval system or transmitted, in any form or by any means without the prior consent of the author, nor be otherwise circulated in any form of binding or cover other than that in which it is published and without a similar condition being imposed on the subsequent purchaser.

www.newgeneration-publishing.com

This book is dedicated to my dear wife, Moraa, and lovely sons Onchoke, Ombuna, Mairura and Omwoyo

Acknowledgement

Special thanks go to my parents, Mr. and Mrs. Oresi, for their support since childhood. I would also like to express my sincere gratitude to my kindred Francisca, Mary, Ambrose, Ernest, Robert Jacqueline and the late James. I am also indebted to the Presbyterian University of East Africa, Kenya Institute of Management, Kisii University Campus, Mount Kenya University, Jomo Kenyatta University of Agriculture & Technology and The Railway Training Institute fraternities for having confidence in me and giving me the chance to exploit my talent. I also wish to thank my workmates, friends and relatives for their constant encouragement and support.

The author, Dr. Samwel Nyagucha Oresi, is an Economist by profession with a bias in Labour Economics and a special interest in Human Resource Management. The liking of HRM is as a result of majoring in Labour Economics. He was born on 21st October 1966 and went to school while still very young. At the age of 4 he was in class 1 at Nyambera DOK (Kisii-Kenya). He later went to Kisii Primary School, from where he did his CPE in 1978. In

1979 he joined Kisii High School, from where he did his KCE in 1982. Having passed with good grades, he went to Kabarnet High School for A-levels and later proceeded to India to pursue a B.A. degree course in Economics. He first joined St. Aloysius College, Jabalpur in 1983. He got his first degree, B.A. Economics, in 1986 from Poona University. He then completed his M.A. Economics in 1988 from Shivaji University. Being only 22 years of age at the time, and on the advice of his father, he decided to pursue his PhD, which he attained in 1994 from Shivaji University at the age of 28.

The author has worked with the Kenya Railways as the Corporate Planning Manager, Supplies & Procurement Manager and Human Resources Officer. He later on moved to lecturing and consultancy, which is his current occupation. The author has published books in Human Resources Management, Macro and Micro Economics, Employee & Industrial Relations and Labour Economics. He has also written question and answer books on economics, labour economics, employee relations &counselling, and research methods.

Foreword

Research is the systematic investigation into and study of materials and sources in order to establish facts and reach new conclusions. It is a systematic investigative process employed to increase or revise current knowledge by discovering new facts. It is divided into two general categories; Basic research which is inquiry aimed at increasing scientific knowledge and Applied research which is effort aimed at using basic research for solving problems or developing new processes, products, or techniques

Research methodology is a science of studying how research is to be carried out. Essentially, the procedures by which researchers go about their work of describing, explaining and predicting phenomena are called research methodology. It is also defined as the study of methods by which knowledge is gained.

The purpose of research is to inform action. Thus, your study should seek to contextualize its findings within the larger body of research. Research must always be of high quality in order to produce knowledge that is applicable outside of the research setting.

Finding reasons why research is important seems like a no-brainer, but many people avoid getting involved in research. The lazy, if not mentally drained, student could say, "Not again." And a disinterested academic could just be doing it for promotion purposes. Yet, for those who like to learn - whether or not they are members of a learning institution - doing research is not just an imperative, but a need. Developing and maintaining undergraduate research programs benefits students, faculty mentors, and the university. Incorporating a research component along with a sound academic foundation enables students to develop independent critical thinking skills along with oral and written communication skills.

The art of work has been made simple to understand and it can be used by diploma, undergraduate and post-graduate students. The writer has also published books on human resource management, economics, labour economics and employee & industrial relations. Other question and answer books written are on Micro & Macro Economics, Labour Economics, and Research Methods. If you have you have any critical review the author can be contacted through; P.O. Box 15785 00100 NRB, Mobiles: 0722857402/0735058551 or Email;

samsamoresi@ymail.com

Test Questions

- Define research and explain the various types of research
- Discuss the qualities of a good research
- Explain the importance of knowing research methods
- Discuss the sources of research topics and the factors considered in choosing a research topic
- Explain the problems facing research
- Define a proposal and explain the characteristics of a good proposal
- Explain the components of a proposal
- Explain the steps used in research
- Discuss the steps used in defining a research problem
- Distinguish between theoretical and conceptual framework
- Discuss the various types of variables
- Explain how research objectives and research questions are formulated
- Explain what you understand by the word "research design" and state the characteristics of a good research design
- Asses the various research designs

- Differentiate between exploratory and descriptive research designs
- Define target population
- Asses the various methods used in sampling
- Define data collection and state the sources of data
- Asses the data collection methods
- Differentiate between validity and reliability
- Explain the process of reporting results
- Asses the various methods of data presentation
- Briefly explain what you understand by the following terms
    - Measure of central tendency
    - Measure for dispersion
    - Range
    - Quartile deviation
    - Mean deviation
    - Standard deviation
    - Measure of relationship
    - Regression
- Correlation
- Explain the basic concept of hypotheses testing
- Explain the steps used in hypothesis testing
- Asses the levels of significance
- Discuss the T-test, F-test and the Chi Square tests
- Asses the importance of computerized data

- Asses the process of preparing a research report
- Explain the process of disseminating a research report
- Explain the ethical issues considered in research
- Explain what you understand by plagiarism
- Discuss the factors that must be considered when making recommendations
- Asses the styles of referencing

CHAPTER ONE
INTRODUCTION

Definition

The word "research" is derived from the Latin word meaning "to know". Research is about asking questions such as:

i) What do I want to know?
ii) How do I want to gain knowledge?
iii) Why do I want to know?

Research may be defined as a disciplined enquiry or systematic investigation aimed at providing solutions to problems. The main purpose of research is to advance or discover new knowledge and improve practice through scientific progress. Research means looking again. To research means to take a more careful look or find out more.

Components of Research

1. Identification of the research area and topic
2. Statement of the problem
3. Literature review
4. Methodology design
5. Sampling frame and sampling techniques
6. Data collection tools, design and techniques
7. Data analysis methods
8. Report writing techniques

Types of Research

Different authors have classified research into various categories.

There are three main types of research:
   i) **Business Research** – This is the systematic and objective process of gathering, recording and analysing data to investigate specific problems to aid in making business decisions
   ii) **Marketing Research** – This is defined as a systematic and objective process of identification, collection of data, analysis and dissemination of information to provide solution to marketing problems
   iii) **Scientific Research** – This is a systematic, controlled, empirical and critical investigation of natural phenomena guided by theory and hypothesis about the presumed relations among such phenomena. It can also be defined as the activity of investigating some phenomena through practices that are consistent with the method of science

Qualitative Research

This includes designs, techniques and measures that do not produce discrete numerical data. Qualitative data can be collected through direct observation, participant observation or interview method. Qualitative research includes an "array of interpretive techniques which seek to describe, decode, translate and otherwise come to terms with the meaning, not the frequency, of certain more or less naturally occurring phenomena in the social world. Qualitative research aims to achieve an in-depth understanding of a situation. Qualitative research is designed to tell the researcher how (process) and why (meaning) things happen as they do. Qualitative techniques are used at both the data collection and data analysis stages of a research project. At the data collection stage, the array of techniques includes focus groups, individual depth interviews, case studies, ethnography, grounded theory, action research and observation". During analysis, the qualitative researcher uses content analysis of written or recorded materials drawn from personal expressions by participants and behavioral observations.

	Qualitative	**Quantitative**
Focus of research	Understand and interpret	Describe, explain and predict
Researcher involvement	High, researcher is participant	Limited, controlled to prevent bias
Research purpose	In-depth understanding theory building	Describe or predict: build and test theory
Sample design	Non-probabilistic purposive	probabilistic
Research design	May involve or adjust during the course of the period often uses multiple methods simultaneously or consistently is not expected involves longitudinal approach	Determined before commencing the project Uses single method or mixed methods Consistency is critical involves either a cross-sectional or a longitudinal approach

Participant preparation	Pre-tasking is common	No preparation desired to avoid biasing the participant.
Date type and preparation	Verbal or pictorial descriptions reduced to verbal codes.	Verbal descriptions reduced to numerical codes for computerized analysis.
Data analysis	Human analysis following computer or human coding	Computerized analysis

Quantitative Research

This includes designs, techniques and measures that produce discreet numerical or quantifiable data.

Advantages of Using both Qualitative and Quantitative Methods

1. Since in many cases a researcher has several objectives, some of these objectives are better assessed using quantitative methods
2. Both methods supplement each other, i.e. qualitative methods provide the in-depth

explanations while quantitative methods provide the data needed to test hypotheses
3. Since both methods have a bias, using both types of research helps to avoid such bias in that each method can be used to check the other

Disadvantages of Using both Qualitative and Quantitative Methods

1. It is expensive
2. Researchers may not have sufficient training in both methods to be able to use them effectively

Classification by Purpose

1. Basic / Pure / Fundamental Research

Basic researchers are interested in deriving scientific knowledge, i.e. they are motivated by intellectual curiosity and do not need to come up with a particular solution. It focuses on generating new knowledge in order to refine or expand existing theories. It does not consider the practical application of the findings to actual problems or situations.

2. Applied Research

Applied research is conducted for the purpose of applying or testing theory and evaluating its usefulness in solving problems. It provides data to support a theory, guide theory revision or suggest the development of a new theory.

3. Action Research

Action research is conducted with the primary intention of solving a specific, immediate and concrete problem in a local setting, e.g. investigating ways of overcoming water shortage in a given area. It is not concerned with whether the results can be generalized to any other setting.

4. Evaluation Research

This is the process of determining whether the intended results were realized.

Types of Evaluation Research

1. Needs Assessment

A need is a discrepancy between an existing set of conditions and a desired set of conditions. The results of needs assessment study provide the foundation for developing new programmes and for making changes in existing ones

2. Formative Evaluation

Helps to collect data about a programme while it is still being developed, e.g. an educational programme, a marketing strategy etc.

3. Summative Evaluation

This is done after the programme has been fully developed. It is conducted to evaluate how worthwhile the final programme has been, especially compared to similar programmes

Classification by Methods of Analysis

1. Descriptive Research

This is the process of collecting data in order to test hypotheses or to answer questions concerning the current status of the subjects in the study. It determines and reports the way things are. It attempts to describe such things as possible behaviour, attitudes, values and characteristics.

Steps Involved In Descriptive Research

   i) Formulating the objectives of a study
   ii) Designing the methods of data collection
   iii) Selecting the sample
   iv) Data collection
   v) Analysing the results

2. Causal-Comparative Research

This is used to explore relationships between variables. It determines reasons or causes for the current status of the phenomenon under study. The variables of interest cannot be manipulated unlike in experimental research.

Steps in Causal-Comparative Research

i) Define the research question
ii) Select a group that possesses the characteristics, which the researcher wants to study
iii) Select a comparison group which does not display the characteristics under study but which is similar to the group in other respects
iv) Collect data on both the experimental and control groups
v) Analyse the data

Advantages of Causal-Comparative Study

i) Allows a comparison of groups without having to manipulate the independent variables
ii) It can be done solely to identify variables worthy of experimental investigation
iii) They are relatively cheap

Disadvantages of Causal-Comparative Study

i) Interpretations are limited because the researcher does not know whether a particular variable is a cause or result of a behaviour being studied
ii) There may be a third variable which could be affecting the established relationship but which may not be established in the study

3. Correlation Method

This describes in quantitative terms the degree to which variables are related. It explores relationships between variables and also tries to predict a subject's score on one variable given his or her score on another variable.

Steps in Correlational Research

i) Problem statement
ii) Selection of subjects
iii) Data collection
iv) Data analysis

Advantages of The Correlational Method

i) Permits one to analyse inter-relationships among a large number of variables in a single study
ii) Allows one to analyse how several variables either singly or in combination might affect a particular phenomenon being studied
iii) The method provides information concerning the degree of relationship between variables being studied

Disadvantages of The Correlational Method

i) Correlation between two variables does not necessarily imply causation, although researchers often tend to interpret such a relationship to mean causation

ii) Since the correlation coefficient is an index, any two variables will always show a relationship even when common sense dictates that such variables are not related
iii) The correlation coefficient is very sensitive to the size of the sample

Classification by Type Of Research
1. Survey Research
A survey is an attempt to collect data from members of a population in order to determine the current status of that population with respect to one or more variables. Survey study is therefore a self-report study, which requires the collection of quantifiable information from the sample. It is a descriptive form of research.

Steps Involved In Survey Research
  i) Problem statement
  ii) Defining objectives
  iii) Selecting a sample
  iv) Preparing the instruments
  v) Data analysis

Purpose of Survey Research

i) It seeks to obtain information that describes existing phenomena by asking individuals about their perceptions, attitudes, behaviour or values
ii) Can be used for explaining or exploring the existing status of two or more variables, at a given point in time
iii) It is the most appropriate to measure characteristics of large populations

Limitations of Survey Research
i) They are dependent on the cooperation of respondents
ii) Information unknown to the respondents cannot be tapped in a survey, e.g. amount saved per year
iii) Requesting information which is considered secret and personal encourages incorrect answers
iv) Surveys cannot be aimed at obtaining forecasts of things to come

2. Historical Research

This involves the study of a problem that requires collecting information from the past.

Purpose of Historical Research

i) Aims at arriving at conclusions concerning causes, effects or trends of past occurrences that may help explain present events and anticipate future events
ii) Attempts to interpret ideas or events that had previously seemed unrelated
iii) Synthesizes old data or merges old data with new historical facts that the researcher or other researchers have discovered
iv) To reinterpret past events that have been studied

Steps Involved In Historical Research
i) Identifying and delineating the problem
ii) Developing hypothesis or hypotheses that one is interested in testing
iii) Collecting and classifying resource materials, determining facts by internal and external criticism
iv) Organizing facts into results
v) Interpreting data in terms of stated hypothesis or theory
vi) Synthesizing and presenting the research in an organized form

3. Observational Research

The current status of a phenomenon is determined not by asking but by observing. This helps to collect objective information.

Steps

i) Selection and definition of the problem
ii) Sample selection
iii) Definition of the observational information
iv) Recording observational information
v) Data analysis and interpretation

Types of Observational Research

1. **Non-participant observation**

    The observer is not directly involved in the situation to be observed

2. **Naturalistic Observation**

    Behaviour is studied and recorded as it normally occurs

3. **Simulation observation**

    The researcher creates the situation to be observed and tells subjects to be observed what activities they are to engage in. Disadvantage; the setting is not natural and the behaviour exhibited by the subjects may not be the behaviour that would occur in a natural setting

4. **Participant observation**

    The observer becomes part of or a participant in the situation. May not be ethical

5. **Case studies**

A case study is an in-depth investigation of an individual, group, institution or phenomenon. It aims to determine factors and relationships among the factors that have resulted in the behaviour under study

6. Content analysis

This involves observation and detailed description of objects, items or things that comprise the sample. The purpose is to study existing documents such as books, magazines in order to determine factors that explain a specific phenomenon

Steps

i) Decide on the unit of analysis
ii) Sample the content to be analysed
iii) Coding
iv) Data analysis
v) Compiling results and interpretations

Advantages

i) Researchers are able to economize in terms of time and money
ii) Errors that arise during the study are easier to detect and correct
iii) The method has no effect on what is being studied

Disadvantages
i) It is limited to recorded communication
ii) It is difficult to ascertain the validity of the data

Qualities of Good Research

1. Clear definition of the research purpose
2. There should be consistency in research focus throughout the research process
3. The research process should be detailed
4. Findings should logically be analysed
5. The research must have an abstract
6. Conclusions should be justified and based on your research findings and not own thoughts
7. Purpose clearly defined: Researcher distinguishes between symptoms of organization's problem, the manager's perception of the problem and the research problem
8. Research process detailed: Researcher provides complete research proposal
9. Research design thoroughly planned: Exploratory procedures are outlined with constructs defined, sample unit is clearly described along with sampling methodology, data collection procedures are selected and designed
10. Limitations frankly revealed: Desired procedure is compared with actual procedure in report, desired

sample is compared with actual sample in the report, impact on findings and conclusions is detailed

11. High ethical standards applied: Safeguards are in place to protect study participants, organizations, clients and researchers. Recommendations do not exceed the scope of the study. The study's methodology and limitations sections reflect researcher's restraint and concern for accuracy
12. Findings presented unambiguously: Findings are clearly presented in words, tables and graphs. Findings are logically organized to facilitate reaching a decision about the manager's problem. Executive summary of conclusions is outlined. Detailed table of contents is tied to the conclusions and findings presentation
13. Conclusions justified: Decision-based conclusions are matched with detailed findings
14. Researcher's experience reflected: Researcher provides experience / credentials with report
15. Adequate analysis for decision-makers' needs: sufficiently detailed findings are tied to collection instruments

Importance of Knowing Research Methods

i) Increased effectiveness of solving problems in analytical context
ii) Improved ability to understand and effectively apply the findings of the research
iii) Enhanced ability to access what is made by others
iv) Increased capacity to evaluate the soundness of theories

Choosing a Research Topic

1. Choose a topic that is appealing to you. Self-interest must come first
2. The topic must be appropriate for the course so as to help you expand your knowledge on the subject matter
3. The topic must be specific
4. Choose a topic that has sufficient material available, e.g. reading material
5. Topic should be within the time recommended
6. Financial ability should be considered
7. Avoid topics that are highly controversial, e.g. religion
8. Avoid topics that are oversized
9. Avoid topics that are trivial
10. Avoid recycling

Sources of Topics
i) Area of interest
ii) Reference sources
iii) Current periodicals
iv) Browsing the library collection and internet

Problems Facing Research
1. Research is a costly undertaking
2. Research process takes a lot of time
3. We have very few professional researchers
4. Language barriers
5. Geographical coverage
6. Negative attitude by most characters
7. Lack of literature
8. Government regulations

Review Questions
i) Define research and explain the various types of research
ii) Discuss the qualities of good research
iii) Explain the importance of knowing research methods
iv) Discuss the sources of research topics and the factors considered in choosing a research topic
v) Explain the problems facing research

CHAPTER TWO
WRITING A RESEARCH PROPOSAL

Definition of a Proposal

A research proposal is also known as a work plan, an outline, a draft plan, statement of intent or a prospectus. A proposal tells us what, why, how, where, and on whom the study will be done. It must also show the benefits of the research/study. A research proposal is essentially a road work showing clearly the location from which the journey begins, the destination to be reached and the methods to be used to reach there. Every research must have a sponsor and thus the sponsor must understand the research/project. The sponsor may be the lecturer for students, firms, universities, Government, etc.

Significance of a Research Proposal

i) It serves as a summary of major decisions in a research process

ii) Serves as a written agreement between the researcher and the sponsor, e.g. on geographical scope and time scope

iii) It is used to solicit for funds

iv) It helps in thinking through the project

v) Resolves any future misunderstandings

Characteristics of a Good Proposal

Generally a good proposal should be:

1. Clear/neat
2. Convincing
3. Detailed
4. Reliable
5. Data based
6. Realistic
7. Systematic in focus
8. Time bound

Other considerations will be:
1. The need for the proposed activity is clearly established, preferably with data
2. The most important ideas are highlighted and repeated in several places
3. The objectives of the project are given in detail
4. There is a detailed schedule of activities for the project, or at least sample portions of such a complete project schedule
5. Collaboration with all interested groups in planning of the proposed project is evident in the proposal
6. The commitment of all involved parties is evident, e.g., letters of commitment in the appendix and cost

sharing stated in both the narrative of the proposal and the budget

7. The budget and the proposal narrative are consistent
8. The uses of money are clearly indicated in the proposal narrative as well as in the budget
9. All of the major matters indicated in the proposal guidelines are clearly addressed in the proposal
10. The agreement of all project staff and consultants to participate in the project was acquired and is so indicated in the proposal
11. All governmental procedures have been followed with regard to matters such as civil rights compliance and protection of human subjects
12. Appropriate detail is provided in all portions of the proposal
13. All of the directions given in the proposal guidelines have been followed carefully
14. Appendices have been used appropriately for detailed and lengthy materials which the reviewers may not want to read but are useful as evidence of careful planning, previous experience, etc.
15. The length is consistent with the proposal guidelines and/or funding agency expectations
16. The budget explanations provide an adequate basis for the figures used in building the budget

17. If appropriate, there is a clear statement of commitment to continue the project after external funding ends
18. The qualifications of project personnel are clearly communicated
19. The writing style is clear and concise. It speaks to the reader, helping the reader understand the problems and proposal. Summarizing statements and headings are used to lead the reader

Types of Proposals

i) **Academic proposal** – This type of proposal is found in academic institutions

ii) **Funding proposal** – This is commonly used by NGOs to solicit for funds

iii) **Business bidding proposal** – This is used by business people to bid for tenders

iv) **Business proposal** – This type of proposal is also known as a business plan. It is used by potential investors or public institutions to get approval

Contents of a Proposal
Preliminary Pages

1. Title page
2. Declaration
3. Dedication

4. Acknowledgement
5. Abstract
6. Table of Contents
7. List of Tables
8. List of Figures
9. Abbreviations/Acronyms
10. Definition of Terms

Main Text

i) *Chapter One* – This contains the Introduction to the Study and should have Introduction, Background of the Study, Statement of the Problem, Objectives of the Study (General and Specific), Research Questions, Significance/Importance of the Study, Limitations of the Study and Scope of the Study

ii) *Chapter Two* – This deals with Literature Review and should have Introduction, Review of Theoretical Literature, Critical Review, Summary and Conceptual/Theoretical Framework

iii) *Chapter Three* – This captures the Research Design and Methodology and should give the Introduction, Research Design, Target Population, Sampling Technique, Data Collection Methods and Data Analysis/Presentation Methods

iv) *References* – All the authors and books used in the text should appear in the references. Use the recommended style of referencing but usually it is the APA style of referencing

Appendices

i) Letter of Introduction
ii) Questionnaire
iii) Budget
iv) Time Frame

Review Questions

i) Define a proposal and explain the characteristics of a good proposal
ii) Explain the components of a proposal

CHAPTER THREE
PROCESS OF RESEARCH

Research Process/Steps

The research process is the sequence of steps in the design and implementation of a research study from problem formulation to research report writing. The research process begins when a management dilemma triggers the need for a decision. For example, a growing number of complaints about post-purchase service can start the process. Such an event will cause the manager to reconsider their purposes or objective, define a problem for solutions, or develop strategies for solutions they have identified. The stages in the research process include the following:

i) Formulate research problem
ii) Development of an approach to the problem
iii) Research design formulation
iv) Field work or data collection
v) Analyse and interpret data
vi) Report preparation and presentation

Identification of Research Area

The research process starts by formulating a research problem that can be investigated through research procedures.

Identifying a Research Problem

The first step in selecting a research problem is to identify the broad area that one is interested in. Such an area should be related to the professional interests and goals of the researcher, e.g. low-cost housing, productivity of workers, small-scale businesses etc. The second step is to identify a specific problem within it that will form the basis of the research study. The research problem should be an important one, i.e. it should:

i) Lead to findings that have widespread implications in a particular area
ii) Challenge some commonly held truism
iii) Review the inadequacies of existing laws, views or policies
iv) Cover a reasonable scope, e.g. not too narrow or too general

A research problem is the basic management or societal challenge or opportunity, which motivates a piece of research. A problem well defined is said to be a problem half solved. This is why a researcher needs to identify and describe a research problem with great precision. In defining the problem, the researcher should take into account the purpose of the study and the relevant background information needed. Before a researcher sets out to carry on research there should be an issue or a problem that is to be investigated.

A research problem has some conditions to be met:

i) There must be an individual/ group/ organization to which the problem can be attributed
ii) There must be at least two cause of action to be pursued. A cause of action is defined by one or more values of the controlled variables
iii) There must be two or more possible outcomes emanating from the cause of action. There must be a preferable outcome

The causes of action available must prove same chance of obtaining the objective but they cannot provide the same chance, otherwise the choice could not matter; thus, a *research problem* can be defined as a matter of concern/issue under investigation in order for the researcher to come up with solutions to it or just findings in case it is not a problem.

A useful way to approach the research process is to state the basic dilemma that prompts the research and then try to develop other questions by progressively breaking down the original question into more specific ones. Management dilemma is usually a symptom of an actual problem, such as: rising cost, declining sales, increasing employee turnover in a restaurant, an increasing number of letters and phone complaints about post purchase and a large number of product defects during the manufacture of an automobile. The manager and research collaborator have to define the following:

i) *Management decision*: A restatement of the manager's dilemma(s) in question form

ii) *Research questions*: The hypothesis that best states the objective of the research, the question(s) that focuses the researcher's attention

iii) *Investigative questions*: Questions the researcher must answer to satisfactorily answer the research questions, what the manager feels he needs to know to arrive at a conclusion about the management dilemma

iv) *Measurement questions*: What participants in research are asked or what specifically is observed in a research study

Defining the Research Problem

A research problem refers to some difficulty which the researcher experiences in the context of either a theoretical or practical situation and wants to obtain a solution for. A research problem exists if the following conditions are met:

i) There must be an individual or a group which has some difficulty or problem

ii) There must be some objective(s) to be attained

iii) There must be alternative means or courses of action for obtaining the objective(s) one wishes to attain
iv) There must be some doubt in the mind of a researcher with regard to the selection of alternatives
v) There must be some environment(s) to which the difficulty pertains

Certain factors determine the scope of a research study and these include:
i) The time available to carry it out
ii) The money available to carry it out
iii) The availability of equipment (if needed) to carry it out
iv) The availability of subjects or the units of study

Steps in Defining Research Problem

This involves the task of laying down boundaries within which a researcher will study the problem with a predetermined objective in view. The following steps can be followed:

1. *Start with a general statement of the problem.* At this stage the research problem is stated in a broad way, putting scientific or intellectual interest into consideration. A researcher should at this stage read

thoroughly in the area of interest. Some preliminary survey might be necessary and the researcher can also seek expert help

2. *Understand the nature of the problem.* This step helps to understand the origin and nature of the problem. The researcher should analyse what made him raise the topic or discuss the problem with those who have more knowledge about it

3. *Surveying the available literature.* This process is also known as literature review, where the researcher goes through all the relevant journals, books, newspaper articles; this will help him know if there are certain gaps in the theory, or whether the existing theories applicable to the problem under study are consistent with each other, or whether the findings of a different study do not follow a pattern consistent with the theoretical expectation

4. *Developing ideas through discussion.* Discussion helps in discovering new ideas and development of different perceptions of the problem being looked at. It is advisable that a researcher discusses the problem with colleagues and other experts who have knowledge in the same area

5. *Rephrasing the research problem.* Finally, the researcher should rephrase the problem into a

working condition. Once the nature of the problem has been understood, rephrasing the problem should be an easy task. By rephrasing, the researcher puts research problem in as specific terms as possible so that it becomes operational and helps in the development the hypothesis

6. The researcher should keep in view the environment within which the problem is to be studied and understood
7. Technical terms and words or phrases with special meanings used in the statement of the problem, should be clearly defined
8. Basic assumptions or postulates (if any) relating to the research problem should be clearly stated
9. A straightforward statement of the value of the investigation should be provided
10. The suitability of the time period and the sources of data available must also be considered by the researcher in defining the problem
11. The scope of the investigation, or the limits within which the problem is to be studied, must be mentioned explicitly in defining a research problem

Selecting the Problem

The following points must be observed by a researcher in selecting a research problem or a subject of study:
i) A subject which is overdone should not be normally chosen, for it will be a difficult task to throw any new light in such a case
ii) A controversial subject should not become the choice of an average researcher
iii) Too narrow or too vague problems should be avoided
iv) The subject selected for research should be familiar and feasible so that the related research material or sources of research are within one's reach
v) The importance of the subject, the qualifications and the training of a researcher, the costs involved and the time factor must be considered
vi) The selection of a study must be preceded by a preliminary study

Ways of Identifying a Specific Research Problem from the Broad Area

i) Existing theories
ii) Existing literature
iii) Discussions with experts
iv) Previous research studies
v) Replication
vi) The media

vii) Personal experience

Stating the Problem

A research study starts with a brief introductory section. The researcher introduces briefly the general area of study, and then narrows down to the specific problem to be studied

Characteristics of a Good Problem Statement

i) It should be written clearly and in such a way that the reader's interest is captured immediately
ii) The specific problem identified in the problem statement should be objectively researchable
iii) The scope of the specific research problem should be indicated
iv) The importance of the study in adding new knowledge should be stated clearly
v) The problem statement must give the purpose of the research

Stating the Purpose

The purpose of a study crystallizes the researcher's inquiry into a particular area of knowledge in a given field. If the purpose is accurately expressed, the research process will be carried out with ease. The purpose of the study should meet the following criteria:

i) It must be indicated clearly, unambiguously and in a declarative manner
ii) The purpose should indicate the concepts or variables in the study
iii) Where possible, the relationships among the variables should be stated
iv) The purpose should state the target population
v) The variables and target population given in the purpose should be consistent with the variables and target population operationalized in the methods section of the study

In stating the purpose of the study, the researcher should choose the right words to convey the focus of the study effectively. Use of subjective or biased words or sentences should be avoided.

Examples

Biased	Neutral
To show	To determine
To prove	To compare
To confirm	To investigate
To verify	To differentiate
To check	To explore
To demonstrate	To find out
To indicate	To examine
To validate	To inquire
To explain	To establish
To illustrate	To test

Stating the Objectives

Research objectives are those specific issues within the scope of the stated purpose that the researcher wants to focus upon and examine in the study.

Characteristics of a Good Objective
  i) Specific
  ii) Measurable
  iii) Achievable
  iv) Reliable
  v) Time bound

Objectives guide the researcher in formulating testable hypotheses. In stating the objectives of the study, the researcher should choose the right words to convey the focus of the study effectively. Use of subjective or biased words or sentences should be avoided

Literature Review

The review of literature involves the systematic identification, location and analysis of documents containing information related to the research problem being investigated It should be extensive and thorough because it is aimed at obtaining detailed knowledge of the topic being studied. Literature review is the documentation of a comprehensive review of the published and unpublished work from secondary sources of data in the area of specific interest to the researcher.

Purpose of literature review

1. To determine what has already been done related to the research problem being studied. This will help the researcher to:
    i) Avoid unnecessary and unintentional duplication
    ii) Form the framework within which the research findings are to be interpreted
    iii) Demonstrate his or her familiarity with the existing body of knowledge

2. Helps reveal the strategies, procedures and measuring instruments that have been found useful in investigating the problem in question. This will help the researcher to:
   i) Avoid mistakes that have been made by other researchers
   ii) Benefit from other researcher's experiences
   iii) Clarify how to use certain procedures, which one may only have learned in theory
3. Helps to suggest other procedures and approaches, which will help, improve the research study
4. Familiarizes the researcher with previous studies, which facilitates interpretation of the results of the study. If there is a contradiction, the literature review might provide rationale for the discrepancy
5. It helps the researcher to limit the research problem and to define it better
6. Helps to determine new approaches and stimulates new ideas. The researcher may be alerted to research possibilities, which have been overlooked in the past
7. Approaches that have been proved to be futile will be revealed through the literature review
8. Specific suggestions and recommendations for further research can be found by reviewing the literature

9. It pulls together, integrates and summarizes what is known in an area, thus helping to reveal gaps in information and areas where major questions still remain

Steps in Carrying Out the Literature Review

1. Familiarize yourself with the library before beginning the literature review
2. Make a list of key words or phrases to guide your literature search
3. With the key words and phrases related to the study, one should go to the source of literature
4. Summarize the references on cards for easy organisation of the literature
5. Once collected, the literature should be analysed, organized and reported in an orderly manner
6. Make an outline of the main topics or themes in order of presentation
7. Analyse each reference in terms of the outline made and establish where it will be most relevant
8. The literature should be organized in such a way that the more general is covered first before the researcher narrows down to that which is more specific to the research problem

Sources of Literature

1. *Primary sources*: are direct descriptions of any occurrence by an individual who actually observed or witnessed the occurrence
2. *Secondary source*: they include any publications written by an author who was not a direct observer or participant in the events described

Examples
1. Scholarly journals
2. Theses and dissertations
3. Government documents
4. Papers presented at conferences
5. Books
6. References quoted in books
7. International indices
8. Abstracts
9. Periodicals
10. The Africana section of the library
11. Reference section of the library
12. Grey literature
13. Inter-library loan
14. The British lending library
15. The internet
16. Microfilm

Importance of the Literature Review

1. The main purpose of the literature review is to determine what has been already related to the research being studied, so as to avoid unnecessary and unintentional duplication and also form the framework within which the research findings are to be interpreted
2. A review of the literature will reveal what strategies, procedures and measuring instruments have been found useful in investigating the problem in question. This information helps one to avoid mistakes that have been made by other researchers and also helps to benefit from other researchers' experiences
3. In most cases the literature review will suggest other procedures and approaches. This is very useful information because a researcher could try out suggested approaches, especially if they will improve the research study
4. It enables the researcher to be familiar with previous studies and thus facilitate interpretation of the result of the study
5. Reviewing the literature critically will provide the foundation on which your research is built. The main purpose of the literature review is to help you to develop a good understanding and insight into

relevant previous research and the trends that have emerged

6. The precise purpose of your reading of the literature will influence the approach you are intending to use in your research. For some research projects you will use the literature to help you to identify theories and ideas that you will test, using data. This is known as *deductive approach*, in which you develop a theoretical or conceptual framework, which you subsequently test using data

7. For other research projects you will be planning to explore your data and to develop theories from them that you will subsequently relate to the literature. This is known as the *inductive approach* and, although your research still has a clearly defined purpose with research question(s) and objectives, you do not start with any predetermined or conceptual frameworks. Such an approach cannot be taken without a conceptual knowledge of your subject area. It is however, impossible to review every single piece of the literature before collecting your data

8. The purpose of your literature review is not to provide a summary of everything that has been written on your research topic, but to review the most relevant and significant research on your topic

Your review also has a number of other purposes. Many of these have been highlighted by Gall et al. (2002) in their book for students undertaking education research and are:

i) To help you refine further your research question(s) and objectives

ii) To highlight research possibilities that has been overlooked implicitly in research to date

iii) To discover explicit recommendations for further research. These can provide you with a superb justification for your own research question and objectives

iv) To help you to avoid simply repeating work that has been done already

v) To sample current opinions in newspapers, professional and trade journals, thereby gaining insights into the aspect of your research questions and objectives that are considered newsworthy

vi) To discover and provide an insight into research approaches, strategies and techniques that may be relevant to your own research questions and objectives

Steps in the Literature Review

1. Be familiar with the literature before beginning the literature review

2. Make a list of key words or phrases to guide your literature search. For example, if the study deals with family conflict, other phrases that could be used to search the literature are family, family violence, abuse or family Dissolution
3. With the key words and phrases related to the study, one should go to the source literature. Library staff are generally very helpful in offering guidance
4. Summarize the references on cards for easy organization of the literature
5. Once collected, the literature should be analysed, organized and reported in an orderly manner. Such organization, analysis and reporting represents the hardest part of the literature review
6. Make an outline of the main topics or themes in order of presentation. Decide on the number of headlines and sub-headlines required depending on how detailed the review is
7. Analyse each reference in terms of the outline made and establish where it will be most relevant
8. Studies contrary to received wisdom should not be ignored when reviewing literature. Such studies should be analysed and a possible explanation for the differences given
9. The literature should be organized in such a way that the more general is covered first before the

research narrows down to that which is more specific to the research problem. Organizing the literature in this way leads to a testable hypothesis

10. Some researchers prefer to have a brief summary of the literature and its implications. This is however, optional depending on the length of the literature under review

Scope of the Literature Review

i) If the area of study has been studied for a long time and there is a huge body of literature, one can read only those studies that are reasonably close to one's research topic. In those thoroughly explored areas, much greater depth is available and the researcher can personally cover a narrower topic range of greater depth

ii) In new or little researched areas, where little depth is available, a researcher would require to review any relevant material in order to develop a logical framework for the study and appropriate hypothesis for the study

iii) A researcher should avoid the temptation to include all available materials. Excessive material does not mean greater information. A smaller, well organized review is preferable to a review containing many studies that are remotely related to the problem

Evaluating Information Sources

Researchers evaluate and select information sources based on five factors that can be applied to any type of source, whether printed or electronic. These are:

i) Purpose: The purpose is what the author is trying to accomplish, e.g. to enlighten, to define terms, to entertain etc.

ii) Scope: what is the date of publication? What time period does this source cover? How much of the topic is covered and to what depth? Is the material covered local, regional or international?

iii) Authority: The author and the author's credentials should be given both in printed and electronic sources

iv) Audience: When evaluating the plausible audience of a source, look for key indicators including vocabulary, types of information and questions or directions that guide the search

v) Format: This relates to how the information is presented and how easy it is to find a specific piece of information

Tips on Good Review of Literature

i) Do not conduct a hurried review for fear of overlooking important studies
ii) Do not rely too heavily on secondary sources
iii) Check daily newspapers as they contain very educative, current information
iv) Copy the references correctly in the first place so as to avoid the frustration of trying to retrace a reference later
v) Do not only concentrate on findings, check on methodology and measurement of variables

General Rules of Citation

i) Every paragraph must have a source
ii) Use the American Psychological Association (APA) publication style
iii) Citation includes only surname and year. When starting with author the year is bracketed e.g. "According to Kotler (2013) a research design..." At the end of a sentence both surname and year in brackets eg "...descriptive research design is used" (Mugenda and Mugenda, 2013).
iv) When citing more than two authors, use one surname and the Latin words *et al*, meaning and others

v) For authors with the same surname include the initials
vi) For corporate authors cite the name once and thereafter use abbreviations

Content of the Critical Review

As you begin to find, read and evaluate the literature, you will need to think how to combine the academic theories and ideas about which you are reading to form the critical review that will appear in your project report. Your review will need to evaluate the research that has already been undertaken in the area of your research project, show and explain the relationship between published research findings and reference the literature in which they were reported.

It will draw out the key points and trends (recognizing any omissions and bias) and present them in a logical way which also shows the relationship to your own research. In doing so you will also provide readers of your project research with the necessary background knowledge to your research questions and objectives and establish the boundaries of your own research.

It will also enable readers to see your ideas against the background of previous published research in the area.

Critique of Theories

This means appraising or evaluating a problem with effective use of language. It emphasizes the need of you as the reviewer, to use own skill both of making reasoned judgments and of arguing effectively in writing.

Critique of Tradition

This includes your questioning, where justification exists to do so, the conventional wisdom, the *"critique of authority"*. Finally it is likely to include recognizing in your review the knowledge and information you are discussing are not value free, *"The Critique of objectivity"*.

Evaluating whether your Literature review is Critical

1. Have you shown how your research questions relate to previous research reviewed?
2. Have you assessed the strengths and weaknesses of the research reviewed?
3. Have you been objective in your discussion and assessment of other people's research?
4. Have you included references to research that are counter to your own opinion?
5. Have you distinguished clearly between facts and opinions?

6. Have you made reasoned judgments about the values and relevance of others' research to your own?
7. Have you justified clearly your own ideas?
8. Have you highlighted those areas where new research (yours) is needed to provide fresh insights and taken these into account in your arguments?
    i) Where there are inconsistencies in current knowledge and understanding?
    ii) Where there are omissions or bias in published research?
    iii) Where research findings need to be tested further?
    iv) Where evidence is lacking, inconclusive, contradictory or limited?
9. Have you justified your arguments by correctly referencing published research?

Theoretical Framework

After conducting the interviews, completing a literature survey, and defining the problem, one is ready to develop a theoretical framework. A theoretical framework is a conceptual model of how one theory makes logical sense of the relationships among the several factors that have been identified as important to the problem. The theoretical framework discusses the interrelationships among the variables that are deemed to be integral to the dynamics of the situation being investigated.

Developing such a framework helps us to postulate or hypothesize and test certain relationships and thus to improve our understanding of the dynamic of the situation. From the theoretical framework, then, a testable hypothesis can be developed to examine whether the theory formulated is valid or not. Thus, the entire research rests on the basis of the theoretical framework. Good theoretical research is central to examining the problem under investigation.

Conceptual Framework

A conceptual framework is defined as "a set of broad ideas and principles taken from relevant fields of enquiry and used to structure a subsequent presentation" (Reichel and Ramney, 1987). It explains either graphically or in narrative form the main dimensions being studied, or the presumed relationships among them. It is a framework showing the relationship between the independent variables and the dependant variable.

Variables

A variable is anything that can take on differing values. The values can differ at various times for the same object or person, or at the same time for different objects or persons. A variable is a measurable characteristic that assumes different values among the subjects. Examples of variables are units, absenteeism and motivation.

Types of Variables

1. Dependent Variable/Criterion Variable

This is the variable of primary interest to the researcher. The researcher's goal is to understand and describe the dependent variable, to explain its variability or to predict it. It is the main variable that lends itself for investigation as a viable factor. Through the analysis of the dependent variable (that is, finding what variable influences it) it is possible to find answers or solutions to the problem. It is the variable that is measured, predicted or monitored and is expected to be affected by manipulation of an independent variable. It indicates the total influence arising from the effects of the independent variable. It varies as a function of the independent variable, e.g. influence of hours studied on performance in a statistical test, influence of distance from the supply centre on the cost of building materials.

2. Independent Variable/Predictor Variable

This is the variable that influences the dependent variable in either a positive or negative way. The variable in the dependent variable is accounted for by the independent variable. It is a variable that a researcher manipulates in order to determine its effect or influence on another variable. It predicts the amount of variation that occurs in other variables.

Types of independent variables

i) **Experimental variables:** These are variables which the researcher has manipulative control over. They are commonly used in biological and physical sciences, e.g. influence of amount of fertilizer on the yield of wheat, influence of alcohol on reaction time

ii) **Measurement types of independent variables:** These are variables which have already occurred. They have fixed manipulative and uninfluenceable properties. Most of the variables are either environmental or personalogical, e.g. age, gender, marital status, race, colour, geographical location, nationality, soil type, altitude etc. (e.g. influence of nationality on choice of food)

3. Moderating Variable

This is a variable that has a strong contingent effect on the independent variable-dependent variable relationship. That is, the presence of a third variable (the moderating variable) modifies the original relationship between the independent and dependent variables.

4. Intervening Variable

This is the variable that surfaces between the times the independent starts operating to influence the dependent variable and the time their impact is felt on it. There is thus a temporal quality or time dimension to the intervening variable. The intervening variable surfaces as a function of the independent variable operating in any situation, and helps to conceptualize and explain the independent variable on the dependent variable. They are a special case of extraneous variables. The difference between the intervening and extraneous variables is in the assumed relationship among the variables. An intervening variable is a hypothetical internal state that is used to explain relationships between observed variables, such as independent and dependent variables, in empirical research. With an extraneous variable, there is no causal link between the independent and dependent variable, but they are independently associated with a third variable – the extraneous variable. An intervening variable is recognized as being caused by the independent variable and as being a determinant of the dependent variable.

Independent ⟶ intervening ⟶ dependent

The total effect of an independent variable on a dependent variable can be subdivided into direct and indirect effects:
i) Indirect effects are those effects of an intervening variable

ii) Direct effects are not transmitted through another variable

The choice of the right intervening variables helps one not only to determine accurately the total effects of an independent variable on the dependent variable but also partition the total effects into direct and indirect. Examples of intervening variables include: motivation, intelligence, intention, and expectation.

5. Extraneous Variable

These are independent variables that are not related to the purpose of study but may affect the dependent variables. For example, a researcher may test the hypothesis that there is a relationship between children's gain in social study achievement and self-concepts. In this case self-concept is an independent variable and social achievement is a dependent variable But intelligence may well affect social study achievement and is thus termed as an extraneous variable. They are those variables that affect the outcome of a research study, either because the researcher is not aware of their existence or, if the researcher is aware, she or he has no control over them.

Extraneous variables are often classified into four types:

i) **Subject variables:** These are the characteristics of the individuals being studied that might affect their actions. These variables include age, gender, health status, mood, background, etc.

ii) **Experimental variables:** These are characteristics of the persons conducting the experiment which might influence how a person behaves. Gender, the presence of racial discrimination, language, or other factors may qualify as such variables

iii) **Situational variables:** These are features of the environment in which the study or research was conducted, which have a bearing on the outcome of the experiment in a negative way. Included are the air temperature, level of activity, lighting, and the time of day

iv) **Control Variables/Concomitant/Covariate or Blocking Variables:** These are extraneous variables that are built into the study. Extraneous variables are variables that influence the results of a study when they are not controlled

Reasons for introducing control variables:

a) It increases the validity of the data

b) It leads to more convincing generalizations

Since absolute control of extraneous variables is not possible in any study, results are interpreted on the basis of degrees of confidence rather than certainty.

Once the major extraneous variables are identified, the researcher can control them by:

i) Building the extraneous variable into the study: i.e. including it as an independent variable. E.g. in determining the effect of alcohol on reaction time, sex may influence reaction time. Therefore, sex can be introduced as an independent variable. Using regression, one can measure the effect of alcohol on reaction time, controlling sex

ii) Include them in the study but only at one level, e.g. time is the dependent variable, alcohol level the independent and sex the extraneous variable. Sex can be controlled by sampling only females or males of a given age. The disadvantage of this method is that generalizations are limited to a smaller population

iii) By removing the effects of the extraneous variables by statistical procedures, i.e. by siphoning its effects on the dependent variable. This can be done by analysis of co-variance and partial correlation

6. Antecedent Variables

These do not interfere with the established relationship between an independent and dependent variable but clarify the influence that precedes such a relationship.

Antecedent ⟶ independent ⟶ dependent

Conditions that must hold for a variable to be classified as an antecedent variable:
i) The variables including the antecedent variable must be related in some logical sequence
ii) When the antecedent variable is controlled for, the relationship between the independent and the dependent variables should not disappear. Rather it should be enhanced
iii) When the independent variable is controlled for or its influence removed, there should not be any relationship between the antecedent variable and the dependent variable

Examples include: political stability; attracts investors; increased job opportunities; high standards of living; reduction of poverty

7. Suppressor variable

This is an extraneous variable which when not controlled for, removes a relationship between the two variables. When a suppressor variable is introduced in the study as a control variable, a true relationship emerges

8. Distorter variable

This is a variable that converts what was thought of as a positive relationship into a negative relationship and vice versa. Its effects lead a researcher into drawing erroneous conclusions from the data. When the distorter variable is controlled, a true relationship is obtained. Consideration of distorter variables in a study reduces the chances of making a type I (rejecting a true null hypothesis) or type two (accepting a false null hypothesis) error

9. Exogenous and endogenous variables

These are commonly used in testing hypothesized causal models. Path analysis (a procedure that tests causal links among several variables) is often used in testing the validity of causal relationships in a theory or model

A   C

B   D

C and D are called endogenous variables. Each endogenous variable is caused or explained by the variable that precedes it, e.g. D is caused by A, B and C.

A and B are called exogenous variables. They lack hypothesized causes in the model

Research Objectives

Research objectives are statements that indicate the specific information the researcher seeks to get by conducting a given piece of research. Thus they give a specific guideline to the research work. Research objectives ought to be SMART: Specific, Measurable, Accurate, Realistic and Time bound.

Formulation of Hypothesis/Research Questions

Research Questions

Research questions are refined statements of the specific components of the problem. Research questions ask what specific information is required with respect to the problem components. The research objectives are often converted into research questions that then give a specific direction of the information sought by the researcher.

Research Hypothesis

The research hypothesis is a predictive statement that relates an independent variable to a dependent variable. Usually a research hypothesis must contain at least one independent and one dependent variable. A hypothesis is an unproven statement about a factor or phenomenon that is of interest to the researcher. A hypothesis is also defined as possible answer to the research questions. There are two types of hypotheses; the *null hypothesis* and the *alternative hypothesis*. For example Null Hypothesis: The quantity demanded is determined by price, taste preference and fashion and price of other commodities

Alternative Hypothesis: the quantity demanded is not determined by price, taste preference and fashion and price of other commodities

Unfortunately it is not possible to formulate a hypothesis in all situations; sometimes information is not available to develop hypotheses. It is necessary for every research project to have a hypothesis because they help identify variables to be included in the research design and they form the basis for the empirical test on identified variables.

Research Questions versus Hypothesis

i) Research questions are interrogative while hypotheses are declarative and can be tested empirically

ii) Hypotheses go beyond research questions because they are statements of relationships or propositions rather than merely questions to which answers are sought

iii) Hypotheses suggest variables to be included in research while research question seek to establish the relevance of such variables to research

iv) A hypothesis is a possible answer to a research question

Review Questions

i) Explain the steps used in research

ii) Discuss the steps used in defining a research problem

iii) Distinguish between a theoretical and conceptual framework

iv) Discuss the various types of variables

v) Explain how research objectives and research questions are formulated

CHAPTER FOUR
RESEARCH DESIGN AND METHODOLOGY

Definition of Research Design

Kerlinger (1986) defines research design as the plan and structure of investigation so conceived as to obtain answers to research questions. The plan is the overall scheme or programme of the research. It includes an outline of what the investigator will do from writing hypotheses and their operational implications to the final analysis of data research. Design expresses both the structure of the research problem and the plan of investigation used to obtain empirical evidence on relations of the problem. Therefore research design is the strategy for a study and the plan by which the strategy is to be carried out. It specifies the methods and procedures for the collection, measurement, and analysis of data.

Essentials of Research Design

The design:
1. Is an activity and time based plan
2. Is always based on the research question
3. Guides the selection of sources and types of information
4. Is a framework for specifying the relationships among the study's variables

5. Outlines procedures for every research activity

Classifications of Designs

Research can be classified using eight different descriptors as shown in the table below:

Category	Options
The degree to which the research questions has been crystallized	• Exploratory study • Formal study
The method of data collection	• Monitoring • Interrogation/communication
The power of the researcher to produce effects in the variables in the study.	• Experimental • Ex post facto
The purpose of the study	• Descriptive • casual
The time dimension	• Cross-sectional • longitudinal

The topical scope – breadth and depth of the study	<ul><li>Case</li><li>Statistical study</li></ul>
The research environment	<ul><li>Field setting</li><li>Laboratory research</li><li>simulation</li></ul>
The participants' perception of research activity	<ul><li>Actual routine</li><li>Modified routine</li></ul>

Research Design Formulation

This is the plan according to which research participants are chosen, information collection and data analysis is done. Research design is a framework for conducting the research project. It details the procedures necessary for obtaining the required information and its purpose is to design a study that will successfully validate the hypothesis. It is the conceptual structure within which research is conducted, that is, it consists of the blueprint for collection, measurement and analysis of data. A research design is a master plan/framework or blueprint specifying the methods and procedures of collecting and analysing the needed information. It specifies the details of the procedures necessary for obtaining the information needed to structure or solve the research problems. Thus it pertains to or includes the what, where, when, how much, by what. It basically contains questions as: What is the study all about? Why is the study carried out? Where will the study be carried out? What type of data will be required? What time will it take? Which sample and design will be used? Which data collection techniques will be used? How will data be analysed and how will the report be written?

What Research Design Must Consist of:

i) A clear statement of research problem
ii) Procedures used for gathering information
iii) Population to be studied
iv) Methods to be used in analysing and processing data

Characteristics of Good Research design

i) It should include general terms in broad, economical, efficient, appropriate and flexible language
ii) It should be able to minimize bias and maximize reliability
iii) It should have minimal experimental error

iv) It should yield maximum information and provide opportunity for considering other aspects of the problem. In reality there is no single research which can be said to be appropriate across the board. Much of it will depend on the nature of research at hand. Different research will require different research design

Factors to be Considered when Choosing a Research Design
i) Means of obtaining the information
ii) Availability of skills of researcher and his staff
iii) Objectives of problems to be studied
iv) Nature of problems to be studied
v) Availability of money and time for research

For instance, if a research study is exploratory in nature, where the major emphasis is on discovery of ideas an insights, the research design should be one that allows consideration of many different aspect of a phenomenon. On the other hand, if a study is descriptive in nature, accuracy becomes a major consideration and research design which minimizes bias and maximizes reliability of the evident collected will be used.

Types of Research Design
  1. **Exploratory Research**

Exploratory research design is also known as *Formulative Research Studies*. The main purpose of such a study is that of formulating a problem for more precise investigation or developing a working hypothesis from an operational point of view. The main emphasis in such studies is the discovery of ideas and insights.

Exploration is particularly useful when researchers lack a clear idea of the problems they will meet during the study. Through exploration, researchers develop concepts more clearly, establish priorities, develop operational definitions and improve the final research design. Other factors that necessitate the use of exploration are:

i) To save time and money
ii) If the area of investigation is new
iii) Important variables may not be known or thoroughly defined
iv) Hypotheses for the research may be needed
v) A researcher can explore to be sure if it is practical to do a formal study in the area

Despite its obvious value, researchers and managers give exploration less attention that it deserves. Exploration is sometimes linked to old biases about qualitative research, i.e. subjectivity, non-representativeness and non-systematic design.

When we consider the scope of qualitative research, several approaches are adaptable for exploratory investigations of management questions:

i) In-depth interviewing – usually conversational rather than structured
ii) Participant observation – to perceive first-hand what participants in the setting experience
iii) Films, photographs and videotapes – to capture the life of the group under study
iv) Case studies – for an in-depth contextual analysis of a few events or conditions
v) Document analysis – to evaluate historical or contemporary, confidential or public records, reports, government documents and opinions

Where these approaches are combined, four exploratory techniques emerge with wide applicability for the management researcher:

i) Secondary data analysis
ii) Experience surveys
iii) Focus groups
iv) Two-stage designs

An exploratory research is finished when the researchers have achieved the following:

i) Established the major dimensions of the research task

ii) Defined a set of subsidiary investigative questions that can be used as a guide to a detailed research design
iii) Developed several hypotheses about possible causes of a management dilemma; learned that certain other hypotheses are such remote possibilities that they can be safely ignored in any subsequent study
iv) Concluded additional research is not needed or is not feasible

2. Survey of Literature

This is the most appropriate research design. Hypotheses stated by earlier study may be reviewed and their usefulness evaluated as a basis for further research. It may also be considered whether the already stated hypothesis suggests a new hypothesis. This approach basically entails a survey done in that area and a researcher should also make an attempt to apply concepts or theories developed in different research contexts to the area in which he is working.

3. Experience Survey

This means the survey of people who have experience of the problem to be studied. People who are competent and contribute new ideas are selected to ensure representation of different types of experiences.

4. Analysis of Insight

This is used in areas where there is little experience to serve as a guide. It involves intensive study of issues in the area of interest through the study of existing records or unstructured interviews. The investigator should carry out an intensive study and should possess high skills and techniques in the collection and collating of information.

5. Focus Groups

This is a personal interview conducted simultaneously amongst a small number of individuals. It is more of a discussion than an interview. It is guided by questions directed to the panel to generate data.

6. Descriptive Research

Descriptive study are those which are concerned with describing the characteristics of a particular individual or group, whereas diagnostic research study determines the frequency with which something occurs or its association to something else. Studies concerned with specific predictions, with narration of facts and characteristics concerning individual groups or situations, are termed as descriptive studies. It is the process of collecting data in order to test hypotheses or to answer questions concerning the current status of the subjects in the study. It determines and reports the way things are. Provides answers to questions like Who? What? When? Where? How? It attempts to describe such things as possible behaviour, attitudes, values and characteristics.

7. Cross Sectional Studies/Sample Survey

This is a type of research involving the collection of information from any given sample of the population only once. In single cross sectional design, only one sample of the respondent is drawn from the target population and information is obtained from the sample once. In multiple cross sectional design there are two or more samples of respondents and information from each sample is obtained only once.

8. Cohort Analysis

A cohort analysis is a multiple cross sectional design that has a series of surveys conducted at appropriate time intervals. For example, opinion polls on the best presidential candidate, carried out fortnightly to show the trends overtime. It is of special interest as it is an improved cross sectional design used to monitor system-change in behaviour.

9. Longitudinal Research

This is an investigation involving a fixed sample (panel) of elements that is measured repeatedly over a period of time. The sample remains the same over time, thus providing a series of pictures which, when viewed together, portray a vivid illustration of the situation and changes that are taking place over time. True panels are members studied repeatedly to measure the same variable. Omnibus panel are members studied repeatedly but alongside variables that change,

10. Causal Research

This is used to explore relationships between variables. It determines reasons or causes for the current status of the phenomenon under study. The variables of interest cannot be manipulated, unlike in experimental research.

Advantages of Causal Study

i) Allows a comparison of groups without having to manipulate the independent variables

ii) It can be done solely to identify variables worthy of experimental investigation

iii) They are relatively cheap

Disadvantages of Causal Study
   i) Interpretations are limited because the researcher does not know whether a particular variable is a cause or result of a behaviour being studied
   ii) There may be a third variable which could be affecting the established relationship but which may not be established in the study

11. Correlation Methods

This describes in quantitative terms the degree to which variables are related. It explores relationships between variables and also tries to predict a subject's score on one variable given his or her score on another variable.

Advantages of the correlational method
   i) Permits one to analyse inter-relationships among a large number of variables in a single study
   ii) Allows one to analyse how several variables either singly or in combination might affect a particular phenomenon being studied
   iii) The method provides information concerning the degree of relationship between variables being studied

Disadvantages of the correlational method

i) Correlation between two variables does not necessarily imply causation although researchers often tend to interpret such a relationship to mean causation

ii) Since the correlation coefficient is an index, any two variables will always show a relationship even when common sense dictates that such variables are not related

iii) The correlation coefficient is very sensitive to the size of the sample

Table 4.1 Differences between Exploratory and Descriptive Research

	Exploratory	Descriptive
Overall Design	Flexible	Rigid
Sampling Design	Non-Probability	Probability
Statistical Design	No pre-planned design for analysis	Pre-planned design for analysis
Observational Design	Unstructured instruments for data	Structured instruments for data
Operational Design	No fixed decision about	Advanced decision about

	operational procedure	operational procedures

Sekaran (2006)

Review Questions

i) Explain what you understand by the word "research design" and state the characteristics of a good research design

ii) Asses the various research designs

iii) Differentiate between exploratory and descriptive research designs

CHAPTER FIVE
POPULATION, SAMPLING AND SAMPLING TECHNIQUES

Population

According to Cooper and Schindler (2000) "a population is the total collection of elements about which we wish to make some inferences". A population is a group of individuals, objects or items from which samples are taken for measurement, e.g. a population of students. Population also refers to the group of persons or elements that have at least one thing in common, for instance, students at Mount Kenya University. Population also refers to the larger group from which the sample is taken. In some studies a small group instead of the total population can be studied. It is a complete set of individuals, cases or objects with some observable characteristics.

Sampling Design

A sample design is a definite plan for obtaining subjects from a given population. It refers to the techniques that a researcher adopts in selecting items for the sampling. It lays down the number of items to be included in the sample, that is, the sample size. Sample design is normally determined before data is collected. Sampling is normally done so as to reduce the number of subjects to be studied. It enables a researcher to study all subjects in the population of interest by picking of subjects across a population that has all the characteristics the researcher wishes to study.

It refers to the techniques of the procedure the researcher would adopt in selecting items for the sample.

Factors to Consider in Developing a Sample Design

i) Type of universe; finite or infinite
ii) Sampling unit; geographic: state, district or village, construction unit: house, flat. Social unit: family, club, school or individual
iii) Source list: sampling frame contains all the names of all items of a universe. The list should be comprehensive, correct, reliable and appropriate
iv) The size of the sample. Should be efficient, representative, reliable and flexible
v) Parameters of interest
vi) Budgetary constraints
vii) Sampling procedure

Criteria for Selecting a Sampling Procedure

Two costs are involved in a sampling analysis; i.e. the cost of collecting the data and the cost of an incorrect inference resulting from the data. Two causes of incorrect inferences are systematic bias and sampling error. Systematic bias results from errors in the sampling procedures and it cannot be reduced or eliminated by increasing the sample size. Systematic bias is the result of the following factors:

i) Inappropriate sampling frame
ii) Defective measuring device
iii) Non-respondents
iv) Indeterminacy principle – individuals act differently when kept under observation
v) Natural bias in reporting data, e.g. government tax = downward bias, social organizations = upward bias

Sampling error is the random variations in the sample estimates around a true population parameter. It decreases with the increase in the size of the sample and it happens to be of a smaller magnitude in case of a homogenous population. While selecting a sampling procedure, the researcher must ensure that the procedure causes a relatively small sampling error and helps to control the systematic bias in a better way.

Steps in Sampling Design

Identification of the:

i) Relevant population
ii) Type of universe, i.e. finite or infinite

iii) Parameters of interest
iv) Sampling frame
v) Type of sample, i.e. probabilistic or non-probabilistic
vi) Size of the sample needed

Characteristics of a Good Sample Design

i) Must result in a truly representative sample
ii) Must result in a small sampling error
iii) Must be viable in the context of funds available for the research study
iv) Must ensure that systematic bias is controlled
v) Must be accurate, controlling the degree to which bias is absent from the sample. An unbiased sample is one in which the underestimations and the overestimations are balanced among the members of the sample.
vi) −Must be precise; precision is measured by the standard error estimate of a standard deviation measurement. The smaller the error of the estimate, the higher is the precision of the sample
vii) Must be such that the results of the sample study can be applied in general for the universe with a reasonable level of confidence

The methodology section of a research study describes the procedures that are to be followed in conducting the study. The techniques of obtaining data are developed.

A census is a count of all the elements in a population.

Sample: A sample is a subset of a particular population. The target population is that population to which a researcher wants to generalize the results of the study. There must be a rationale for defining and identifying the accessible population from the target population.

Sampling: the process of selecting a sample from a population.

Reasons for Sampling

i) Cost
ii) Time: Greater speed of data collection
iii) Destructive nature of certain tests
iv) Greater accuracy of results
v) Physical impossibility of checking all items in the population
vi) Availability of population elements

Factors that Influence the Sample Size

i) *Dispersion/variance*: The greater the dispersion or variance within the population, the larger the sample must be to provide estimation precision

ii) *Precision of the estimate*: the greater the desired precision of the estimate, the larger the sample must be
iii) *Interval range*: The narrower the interval range, the larger the sample must be
iv) *Confidence level*: The higher the confidence level in the estimate, the larger the sample must be
v) *Number of subgroups*: The greater the number of subgroups of interest within a sample, the greater the sample size must be, as each subgroup must meet minimum sample size requirements
vi) If the calculated sample size exceeds 5% of the population, sample size may be reduced without sacrificing precision

Types of Sampling Designs /Sampling Procedures

There are two major ways of selecting samples:
1. Probability sampling methods
2. Non-Probability sampling methods

Probability Sampling

This is normally known as random sampling or chance sampling. Under the sampling design every element of the population has an impact on the sample. Samples are selected in such a way that each item or person in the population has a known (Non-zero) likelihood of being included in the sample.

Types of Probability Sampling

Systematic Random Sampling

This involves giving a number to every subject of the population, placing the numbers in a container and picking any number at random. The subjects corresponding to the numbers picked are included in the sample. Another approach is to use the table of random numbers, or random numbers can be generated by computer programs. The items or individuals of the population are arranged in some manner. A random starting point is selected and then every member of the population is selected for the sample.

Advantages

i) Simple to design
ii) Easier to use than the simple random
iii) Easy to determine sampling distribution of mean or proportion
iv) Less expensive than simple random

Disadvantages

i) Periodicity within the population may skew the sample and results

ii) If the population list has a monotonic trend, a biased estimate will result based on the starting point

Simple Random Sampling

A sample is selected so that each item or person in the population has the same chance of being included.

Advantages
  i) Easy to implement with automatic dialling and with computerized voice response systems

Disadvantages
  i) Requires a listing of population elements
  ii) Takes more time to implement
  iii) Uses larger sample sizes
  iv) Produces larger errors
  v) Expensive

Systematic Sampling

Every k^{th} case in the population frame is selected for inclusion in the sample. To obtain a truly random sample all the members of the sampling frame must be randomized.

Stratified Random Sampling

In a stratified sample subjects are selected in such a way that the existing samples in the population are more or less produced in the sample. It means that the sample will consist of more than two samples.

A population is divided into subgroups called strata and a sample is selected from each stratum. After the population is divided into strata, either a proportional or a non-proportional sample can be selected. In a proportional sample, the number of items in each stratum is in the same proportion as in the population, while in a non-proportional sample, the number of items chosen in each stratum is disproportionate to the respective numbers in the population.

Advantages

i) Researcher controls sample size in strata
ii) Increased statistical efficiency
iii) Provides data to represent and analyse subgroups
iv) Enables use of different methods in strata

Disadvantages

i) Increased error will result if subgroups are selected at different rates
ii) Expensive, especially if strata in the population have to be pre-identified

Cluster Sampling

This is used when it is not possible to obtain a sampling frame because the population is either very large or scattered over a large geographical area. It involves the selection of an intact group. The population is divided into internally heterogeneous subgroups and some are randomly selected for further study. A multi-stage cluster sampling method can also be used.

Advantages

i) Provides an unbiased estimate of population parameters if properly done
ii) Economically more efficient than simple random
iii) Lowest cost per sample, especially with geographic clusters
iv) Easy to do without a population list

Disadvantages

i) More error (Lower statistical efficiency) due to subgroups being homogeneous rather the heterogeneous

Multistage Sampling

This is a further development of the principle of cluster sampling. Suppose we want to investigate the working efficiency of insurance firms in Kenya and we want to take a sample of a few insurance firms for this purpose. The first stage is to select a large primary unit such as provinces in a country. This would represent a two-stage sampling design, with the ultimate sampling unit being a cluster of districts. If we select randomly at all stages we will have multi-stage sampling.

Probability Sampling Methods

Non Probability Sampling

This is the sampling procedure which does not afford any basis for estimating the probability that each item in the population has of being included in the sample.

It is used when a researcher is not interested in selecting a sample that is representative of the population.

Convenience Sampling

This is also known as accidental or haphazard sampling. In this method the researcher studies all those persons who are most conveniently available, or who accidentally come into his contact. It involves selecting cases or units of observation as they become available to the researcher, e.g.

asking a question to the radio listeners, roommates or neighbours.

Purposive Sampling/Judgmental Sampling

This is a sampling technique that allows a researcher to use cases that have the required information with respect to the objectives of his study. Cases or subjects are therefore handpicked because they are informative or they possess the required characteristics. This occurs when a researcher selects sample members to conform to some criterion. It allows the researcher to use cases that have the required information with respect to the objectives of his or her study, e.g. educational level, age group, religious affiliation.

Quota Sampling

The researcher purposely selects subjects to fit the quotas identified. The selection of actual participants is not random, since subjects are picked as they fit into identified quotas. The researcher purposively selects subjects to fit the quotas identified e.g.

i) Gender: Male or Female
ii) Class Level: Graduate or Undergraduate
iii) School: Humanities, Science or human resource development
iv) Religion: Muslim, Protestant, catholic, Jewish
v) Fraternal affiliation: member or non-member

vi) Social economic class: Upper, middle or lower

Advantages
i) The main reason why researchers choose **quota** samples is that it allows the researchers to **sample** a subgroup that is of great interest to the study
ii) If a study aims to investigate a trait or a characteristic of a certain subgroup, this type of **sampling** is the ideal technique.

Disadvantages
i) It gives no assurance that the sample is representative of the variables being studied
ii) The data used to provide controls may be outdated or inaccurate
iii) There is a practical limit on the number of simultaneous controls that can be applied to ensure precision
iv) Since the choice of subjects is left to field workers, they may choose only friendly looking people

Snowball Sampling

In this method subjects with the desired characteristics are picked using purposive sampling. The few identified subjects name others that they know have the required characteristics until the researcher gets the number of cases he requires. It is used when the population that possesses the characteristics under study is not well known and can be best located through referral networks. Initial subjects are identified who in turn identify others. Commonly used in drug cultures, teenage gang activities, Mungiki sect, insider trading, Mau Mau etc.

Census

This means using the entire population as the sample. It is very attractive for small populations but very costly for large populations. A census eliminates sampling error and provides data on all the individuals in the population.

Using a Sample from a Similar Study

Another approach is to use the same sample size as those of studies similar to the one you plan to do. There is a risk, though, of repeating errors that were made in determining the sample size for the other research.

Using Published Tables

Published tables are another way of determining the sample size as they provide the sample size for a given set of criteria.

Using Formulas to Calculate Sample Size

Sometimes it is useful to calculate the necessary sample size for a different combination of levels of precision, confidence and variability. It may also be necessary to calculate the precise minimum sample size you require.

Sampling error

This is the difference between a sample statistic and its corresponding population parameter. The sampling distribution of the sample means a probability distribution of possible sample means of a given sample size.

Statistical Inference

Sample information is used to shade some light on population characteristics, i.e. we infer population properties based on findings on the sample. Statistical inference falls into two main areas, i.e. statistical estimation and hypothesis testing.

Statistical Estimation: The characteristics of the sample (sample statistic) are used to estimate or approximate some unknown population characteristics.

Hypothesis testing: The population characteristics are known or assumed. The sample characteristics are used to verify or ascertain this assumed or known population characteristic. The assignment of values to a population parameter based on a sample is called **estimation**. The values assigned to a population parameter based on the value of a sample statistic arre called **an estimate** of the population parameter. The sample statistic used to estimate a population parameter is called **an estimator**. Estimation can be undertaken in two forms, namely, Point estimation or Interval estimation.

Selecting the sample size to estimate a population mean

One of the most common questions asked of statisticians is, how large should the sample taken in a survey be? The answer to this question depends on three factors:

i) The parameter to be estimated

ii) The desired confidence level of the interval estimator

iii) The maximum error of estimation, where error of estimation is the absolute difference between the point estimator and the parameter, e.g. the point estimator

a. of μ is x so that the error of estimation = $x-\mu$

The maximum error of estimation is also called the error bound and is denoted B. Suppose the parameter of interest in an experiment is the population mean μ. The confidence

interval estimator (assuming a normal population, with the population
variance known) is $x + z_{a/2}$ If we want to estimate μ to within certain specified
bound B, we will want the confidence interval estimator to be x+B. As a consequence,

we have $z_{a/2} \dfrac{\sigma}{\sqrt{n}} = B$. Solving for n, we get the following result $n = \dfrac{z_{a/2}^2 \sigma^2}{4n}$

A popular method of approximating is to begin by approximating the range of the random variable. A conservative estimate of 6 is the range divided by 4 i.e. $\sigma \sim Range/4$

This produces a larger value of 6, which results in a larger value of n, which then estimates u with an interval at least as good as was specified.

Examples

i) A production manager would like to estimate the mean time required for workers to complete a task on an assembly line. Assume that she knows that 6 is 80 seconds. How large a sample should she draw to estimate p to within 5 seconds with (i) 90%

confidence (ii) 95% confidence (iii) 99% confidence?

ii) Find n, given that we want to estimate u to within 10 units with 95% confidence, assuming that e = 100

iii) The operations manager of a large production plant would like to estimate the average amount of time a worker takes to assemble a new electronic component. After observing a number of workers assembling similar devices, she noted that the shortest time taken was 10 minutes and longest time taken was 22 minutes. How large a sample of workers should she take if she wants to estimate the mean assembly time to within 20 seconds? Assume that the confidence level is to be 99%.

iv) Determine the sample size necessary to estimate p to within 10 units with 99% confidence. We know that the range of the population is 200 units.

Selecting the Sample Size to Estimate a Population Proportion

i) The manager of a bank feels that 35% of branches will have enhanced yearly collection of deposits after introducing a hike in interest rates. Determine the sample size such that the mean proportion is within plus or minus 0.06 at a confidence level of (i) 90% (ii) 95% and (iii) 99%.

ii) How large a sample should be taken in order to estimate to within 0.01 with 95% confidence? assume that:

    a) You have no information about the value of p

    b) p is believed to be approximately 0.10

    c) p is believed to be approximately 0.90

iii) The director of a management school feels that 55% of students will have enhanced performance if additional input is given to them. Determine the sample size such that the mean proportion is within plus or minus 0.10 at a confidence level of 95%.

Review Questions

i) Define target population

ii) Asses the various methods used in sampling

CHAPTER SIX
METHODS OF DATA COLLECTION

Meaning of Data Collection

Data collection refers to gathering specific information aimed at providing or refuting certain facts. In data collection the researcher must have a clear vision of the instruments to be used. The researcher must also have a clear understanding of what they hope to obtain and how they hope to obtain it.

Sources of Data/Data Collection

Primary Data

This refers to information obtained first hand by the researcher on variables of interest for specific purposes of study. This information is gathered directly from the respondents. It can be qualitative or quantitative research. Primary data can gathered through questionnaires, interviews, focused group discussions observation and experimental studies.

Secondary Data

This is data neither collected by the user nor meant for the user. It involves gathering data that has already been collected by other people. Data is gathered by the collection and analysis of published materials and information from internal sources. It is sometimes known as desk research.

Methods of Primary Data Collection

Questionnaires

A questionnaire is a means of eliciting the feelings, beliefs, experiences, perceptions or attitudes of individuals. It is a combination of questions in written form that is usually sent by post, or online, to the respondents who are expected to answer the questions and return them. Sometimes it can be a walk-in exercise where the questionnaires are handed out in person. As a data collection instrument a questionnaire can be *structured, unstructured* or *semi structured.* A structured questionnaire is one that has closed ended questions. It is restricted and calls for a "yes" or "no" answer. An unstructured questionnaire is one that has open ended questions. It is unrestricted and calls for free responses from the respondent. A semi structured questionnaire has both open and closed ended questions. Each item in the questionnaire is developed to address a specific objective, research question or hypothesis of the study. The researcher must also know how information obtained from each questionnaire item will be analysed.

Advantages
  i) It has a low costs, even when the universe is large and widely spread geographically
  ii) It is free from bias of the interviewer
  iii) Respondents have adequate time to give all the answers
  iv) Uniformity of the questions
  v) Standardized questions

Disadvantages
  i) It has a low rate of return
  ii) Respondent's motivation is difficult to asses
  iii) May present biased samples
  iv) It can only be used when respondents are educated and cooperative
  v) The control of the questionnaire may be lost once it is sent

Types of Questions Used in Questionnaires

1. Structured or Closed-Ended Questions

These are questions accompanied by a list of possible alternatives from which respondents select the answer that best describes their situation.

Advantages of Structured or Closed-Ended Questions

i) They are easier to analyse since they are in an immediately usable form
ii) They are easier to administer
iii) They are economical to use in terms of time and money

Disadvantages of Structured or Closed-Ended Questions

i) They are more difficult to construct
ii) Responses are limited and the respondent is compelled to answer questions according to the researcher's choices

2. Unstructured or Open - Ended Questions

These are questions which give the respondent complete freedom of response. The amount of space provided is always an indicator of whether a brief or lengthy answer is desired.

Advantages of Unstructured or Open - Ended Questions

i) They permit a greater depth of response
ii) They are simple to formulate
iii) The respondent's responses may give an insight into his feelings, background, hidden motives, interest and decisions

Disadvantages of Unstructured or Open - Ended Questions

i) There is a tendency for the respondents to provide information which does not answer the stipulated, research-questions or objectives
ii) The responses given may be difficult to categorize and hence difficult to analyse quantitatively
iii) Responding to open ended questions is time-consuming, which may put some respondents off

3. Contingency Questions

In particular cases, certain questions are applicable to certain groups of respondents. In such cases, follow-up questions are needed to get further information from the relevant sub-group only. These subsequent questions, which are asked after the initial questions, are called 'contingency questions' or 'filter questions'. The purpose of these kinds of questions is to probe for more information. They also simplify the respondent's task, in that they will not be required to answer questions that are not relevant to them.

4. Matrix Questions

These are questions which share the same set of response categories. They are used whenever scales like the Likert scale are being used.

Advantages of Matrix Questions

i) When questions or items are presented in matrix form, they are easier to complete and hence the respondent is unlikely to be put off
ii) Space is used efficiently
iii) It is easy to compare responses given to different items

Disadvantages of Matrix Questions

i) Some respondents, especially the ones that may not be too keen to give the right responses, might form a pattern of agreeing or disagreeing with statements
ii) Some researchers use them when in fact the kind of information being sought could better be obtained in another format

Rules for Constructing Questionnaires and Questionnaire Items

1. List the objectives that you want the questionnaire to accomplish before constructing the questionnaire
2. Determine how information obtained from each questionnaire item will be analysed
3. Ensure clarity and avoid ambiguity
4. If a concept has several meanings and that concept must be used in a question, the intended meaning must be defined
5. Construct short questions where possible

6. Items should be stated as positively as possible
7. Double-barrelled items should be avoided
8. Leading and biased questions should be avoided
9. Very personal and sensitive questions should be avoided
10. Simple words that are easily understandable should be used
11. Questions that assume facts with no evidence should be avoided
12. Avoid psychologically threatening questions
13. Include enough information in each item so that it is meaningful to the respondent

Tips on how to Organize or Order Items in a Questionnaire

1. Begin with non-threatening, interesting items
2. It is not advisable to put important questions at the end of a long questionnaire
3. Have some logical order when putting items together
4. Arrange the questions according to themes being studied
5. If the questionnaire is arranged into content sub-sections, each section should be introduced with a short statement concerning its content and purpose

6. Socio-economic questions should be asked at the end because respondents may be put off by personal questions at the beginning of the questionnaire

Presentation of the Questionnaire
1. Make the questionnaire attractive by using quality paper. It increases the response rate
2. Organize and lay out the questions so that the questionnaire is easy to complete
3. All the pages and items in a questionnaire should be numbered
4. Brief but clear instructions must be included
5. Make your questionnaire as short as possible

Pretesting the Questionnaire

The questionnaire should be pretested with a selected sample, which is similar to the actual sample, which the researcher plans to study. This is important because:

i) Questions that are vague will be revealed in the sense that the respondents will interpret them differently
ii) Comments and suggestions made by respondents during pretesting should be seriously considered and incorporated
iii) Pretesting will reveal deficiencies in the questionnaire

iv) It helps to test whether the methods of analysis are appropriate

Ways of Administering Questionnaires

i) Self-Administered Questionnaires

Questionnaires are sent to the respondents through mail or hand-delivery, and they complete them on their own

ii) Researcher Administered Questionnaires

The researcher can decide to use the questionnaire to interview the respondents. This is mostly done when the subjects may not have the ability to easily interpret the questions, probably because of their educational level

iii) Use of the Internet

The people sampled for the research receive and respond to the questionnaires through their web sites or e-mail addresses

The Letter of Transmittal/Cover Letter

The letter of transmittal/Cover letter should accompany every questionnaire.

Contents of a Letter of Transmittal

i) It should explain the purpose of the study

ii) It should explain the importance and significance of the study
iii) A brief assurance of confidentiality should be included in the letter
iv) If the study is affiliated to a certain institution or organisation, it is advisable to have an endorsement from that institution or organisation
v) In sensitive research, it may be necessary to assure the anonymity of respondents
vi) The letter should contain specific deadline dates by which the completed questionnaire is to be returned

Follow-Up Techniques
i) Sending a follow-up letter which should be polite, and asking the subjects to respond
ii) A questionnaire and a follow-up letter

Response Rate
This refers to the percentage of subjects who respond to questionnaires. Many authors believe that a response rate of 50% is adequate for analysis and reporting. If the response rate is low, the researcher must question the representativeness of the sample.

Factors Affecting Rate of Returned Questionnaires
i) Length of the questionnaire

ii) Reputation of the sponsoring agency
iii) Complexity of the questions asked
iv) Relative importance of the study
v) Quality and design of the questionnaire
vi) Time of the year the questionnaire is distributed

Interviews

This involves presentation of oral-verbal stimuli seeking oral responses. An interview is an oral (face to face) administration of a questionnaire or an interview schedule. To obtain accurate information through interviews, a researcher needs to obtain the maximum co-operation from respondents. Interviews are particularly useful for getting the story behind a participant's experiences. The interviewer can pursue in-depth information around a topic. Interviews may be useful as follow-up to certain respondents to questionnaires, e.g., to further investigate their responses. Usually open-ended questions are asked during interviews. This method can be used through face to face/telephone interviews. It is a conversation in which the roles of the interviewer and the respondent change continually. They may be structured interviews where a guiding questionnaire (interview schedule) is used or an unstructured interview, where there is no questionnaire to be followed. Structured interviews are rigidly standardized and formal, while unstructured interviews are flexible and informal.

Advantages

1. You get more information and in greater depth
2. It can also be applied to record verbal answers to various questions
3. Sample can be controlled
4. Can be used with young children and illiterates
5. Allows the interviewer to clarify questions
6. The language of the interviewer can be adapted to the nature of the respondent
7. The interviewer can collect supplementary information
8. It provides in-depth data, which is not possible to get using a questionnaire
9. It makes it possible to obtain data required to meet specific objectives of the study
10. More flexible than questionnaires because the interviewer can adapt to the situation and get as much information as possible
11. Very sensitive and personal information can be extracted from the respondent
12. The interviewer can clarify and elaborate the purpose of the research and effectively convince respondents about the importance of the research
13. They yield higher response rates

Disadvantages

i) Gaining access to interviewees may be very difficult, especially if they are busy or high-profile people
ii) It is time consuming
iii) They are expensive; e.g. travelling costs
iv) It requires a higher level of skill
v) Interviewers need to be trained to avoid bias
vi) Not appropriate for large samples
vii) Responses may be influenced by the respondent's reaction to the interviewee

Guidelines for Preparation for Interview

1. Choose a setting with little distraction. Avoid loud lights or noises, ensure the interviewee is comfortable (you might ask them if they are), etc. Often, they may feel more comfortable at their own places of work or homes
2. Explain the purpose of the interview
3. Address terms of confidentiality. Note any terms of confidentiality. (Be careful here. Rarely can you absolutely promise anything. Courts may get access to information, in certain circumstances.) Explain who will get access to their answers and how their answers will be analysed. If their comments are to

be used as quotes, get their written permission to do so
4. Explain the format of the interview. Explain the type of interview you are conducting and its nature. If you want them to ask questions, specify if they're to do so as they have them or wait until the end of the interview
5. Indicate how long the interview usually takes
6. Tell them how to get in touch with you later if they want to
7. Ask them if they have any questions before you both get started with the interview
8. Don't count on your memory to recall their answers. Ask for permission to record the interview or bring along someone to take notes

Types of Interviews Approaches

i) Informal, Conversational Interview

No predetermined questions are asked, in order to remain as open and adaptable as possible to the interviewee's nature and priorities; during the interview, the interviewer "goes with the flow".

ii) General Interview Guide Approach

The guide approach is intended to ensure that the same general areas of information are collected from each interviewee; this provides more focus than the conversational approach, but still allows a degree of freedom and adaptability in getting information from the interviewee.

iii) Standardized, Open-Ended Interview

Here, the same open-ended questions are asked to all interviewees (an open-ended question is where respondents are free to choose how to answer the question, i.e., they don't select "yes" or "no" or provide a numeric rating, etc.); this approach facilitates faster interviews that can be more easily analysed and compared.

iv) Closed, Fixed-Response Interview

Here, all interviewees are asked the same questions and asked to choose answers from among the same set of alternatives. This format is useful for those not practiced in interviewing.

Sequence of Questions

1. Get the respondents involved in the interview as soon as possible
2. Before asking about controversial matters (such as feelings and conclusions), first ask about some facts. With this approach, respondents can more easily engage in the interview before warming up to more personal matters

3. Intersperse fact-based questions throughout the interview to avoid long lists of fact-based questions, which tends to leave respondents disengaged
4. Ask questions about the present before questions about the past or future. It's usually easier for them to talk about the present and then work into the past or future
5. The last questions might be to allow respondents to provide any other information they prefer to add and their impressions of the interview

Wording of Questions

1. Wording should be open-ended. Respondents should be able to choose their own terms when answering questions
2. Questions should be as neutral as possible. Avoid wording that might influence answers, e.g. evocative, judgmental wording
3. Questions should be asked one at a time
4. Questions should be worded clearly. This includes knowing any terms particular to the program or the respondent's culture
5. Be careful asking "why" questions. This type of question infers a cause-effect relationship that may not truly exist. These questions may also cause

respondents to feel defensive, e.g. they have to justify their response, which may inhibit their responses to this and future questions

6. While Carrying Out Interview
   a. Occasionally verify the tape recorder (if used) is working
   b. Ask one question at a time
   c. Attempt to remain as neutral as possible. That is, don't show strong emotional reactions to their responses. Patton suggests acting as if "you've heard it all before"
   d. Encourage responses with occasional nods of the head, "uh huh's", etc.
   e. Be careful about the appearance when note taking. That is, if you jump to take a note, it may appear as if you're surprised or very pleased about an answer, which may influence answers to future questions
   f. Provide transition between major topics, e.g., "we've been talking about (some topic) and now I'd like to move on to (another topic)"
   g. Don't lose control of the interview. This can occur when respondents stray to another topic, take so long to answer a

question that time begins to run out, or even begin asking questions to the interviewer

Immediately After Interview

i) Verify if the tape recorder, if used, worked throughout the interview
ii) Make any notes on your written notes, e.g. to clarify any scratching, ensure pages are numbered, fill out any notes that don't make sense, etc.
iii) Write down any observations made during the interview. For example, where did the interview occur and when, was the respondent particularly nervous at any time? Were there any surprises during the interview? Did the tape recorder break?
iv) Creating a non-response sample and weighting results from this sample
v) Substituting another individual for a missing non-participant

Response Error

This occurs when the data reported differ from the actual data. It can occur during the interview or during preparation of data analysis.

1. Participant-initiated error occurs when the participant fails to answer fully and accurately, either by choice or because of inaccurate or

incomplete knowledge. It can be solved by using trained interviewers who are knowledgeable about such problems.

2. Interviewer error can be caused by:
3. Failure to secure full participant cooperation
4. Failure to consistently execute interview procedures
5. Failure to establish appropriate interview environment
6. Falsification of individual answers or whole interviews
7. Inappropriate influencing behaviour
8. Failure to record answers accurately and completely
9. Physical presence bias

Advantages of Personal Interviews

i) Good cooperation from the respondents
ii) Interviewer can answer questions about survey, probe for answers, use follow-up questions and gather information by observation
iii) Special visual aids and scoring devices can be used
iv) Illiterate and functionally illiterate respondents can be reached
v) Interviewer can pre-screen respondent to ensure he / she fits the population profile

vi) Responses can be entered directly into a portable microcomputer to reduce error and cost when using computer assisted personal interviewing

Disadvantages of Personal Interviews
1. High costs
2. Need for highly trained interviewers
3. Longer period needed in the field collecting data
4. Possible wide geographic dispersion
5. Follow-up is labour intensive
6. Not all respondents are available or accessible
7. Some respondents are unwilling to talk to strangers in their homes
8. Some neighbourhoods are difficult to visit
9. Questions may be altered or respondent coached by interviewers

Telephone Interviews
People selected to be part of the sample are interviewed on the telephone by a trained interviewer.

Advantages of Telephone Interviews
1. Lower costs than personal interviews
2. Expanded geographic coverage without dramatic increase in costs

3. Uses fewer, more highly skilled interviewers
4. Reduced interview bias

Personal Interviews

People selected to be part of the sample are interviewed in person by a trained interviewer.

Requirements for Success

Three broad conditions must be met in order to have a successful personal interview:

i) The participant must possess the information being targeted by the investigative questions
ii) The participant must understand his or her role in the interview as the provider of accurate information
iii) The participant must perceive adequate motivation to cooperate

Increasing the Participant's Receptiveness

The first goal in an interview is to establish a friendly relationship with the participant. Three factors will help increase participant receptiveness. The participant must:

i) Believe that the experience will be pleasant and satisfying
ii) Believe that answering the survey is an important and worthwhile use of his or her time

iii) Dismiss any mental reservations that he or she might have about participation

The technique of stimulating participants to answer more fully and relevantly is termed probing. Since it presents a great potential for bias, a probe should be neutral and appear as a natural part of the conversation. Appropriate probes should be specified by the designer of the data collection instrument. There are several probing styles:

i) A brief assertion of understanding and interest, e.g. comments such as "I see", "yes"
ii) An expectant pause
iii) Repeating the question
iv) Repeating the participant's reply
v) A neutral question or comment
vi) Question clarification

Problems likely to be encountered during personal interviews

In personal interviews, the researcher must deal with bias and cost. Biased results are as a result of three types of errors.

Sampling error

This is the difference between a sample statistic and its corresponding population parameter. The sampling distribution of the sample means is a probability distribution of possible sample means of a given sample size.

Non-response error

This occurs when the responses of participants differ in some systematic way from the responses of non-participants. It occurs when the researcher:
i) Cannot locate the person to be studied
ii) Is unsuccessful in encouraging that person to participate

Solutions to reduce errors of non-response are:
iii) Establishing and implementing call-back procedures
iv) Extended completion time
v) Better access to hard-to-reach respondents through repeated call-backs
vi) Use computerized random digit dialling
vii) Responses can be entered directly into a computer file to reduce error and cost when using computer assisted telephone interviewing

Disadvantages of Telephone interviews

1. Response rate is lower than for personal interview
2. Higher costs if interviewing geographically dispersed sample

3. Interview sample must be limited
4. Many phone numbers are unlisted or not working, making directory listings unreliable
5. Some target groups are not available by phone
6. Responses may be less complete
7. Illustrations cannot be used
8. Respondents may not be honest with their responses since it is not a face to face situation

Rules Pertaining to Interviews

The interviewer must

1. Be pleasant
2. Show genuine interest in getting to know respondents without appearing like spies
3. Be relaxed and friendly
4. Be very familiar with the questionnaire or the interview guide
5. Have a guide which indicates what questions are to be asked and in what order
6. Interact with the respondent as an equal
7. Pre-test the interview guide before using it to check for vocabulary, language level and how well the questions will be understood
8. Inform the respondent about the confidentiality of the information given
9. Not ask leading questions

10. Remain neutral in an interview situation in order to be as objective as possible

An Interview Schedule

This is a set of questions that the interviewer asks when interviewing. It makes it possible to obtain data required to meet specific objectives of the study.

Note Taking During Interviews

This refers to the method of recording in which the interviewer records the respondent's responses during the interview.

Advantages

i) It facilitates data analysis since the information is readily accessible and already classified into appropriate categories
ii) If taken well, no information is left out

Disadvantages of Note Taking

i) It may interfere with the communication between the respondent and the interviewer
ii) It might upset the respondent if the answers are personal and sensitive
iii) If it is delayed, important details may be forgotten
iv) It makes the interview lengthy and boring

Tape Recording

The interviewer's questions and the respondent's answers are recorded either using a tape recorder or a video tape.

Advantages

i) It reduces the tendency for the interviewer to make unconscious selection of data in the course of the recording
ii) The tape can be played back and studied more thoroughly
iii) A person other than the interviewer can evaluate and categorize responses
iv) It speeds up the interview
v) Communication is not interrupted

Disadvantages

i) It changes the interview situation since some respondents become nervous
ii) Respondents may be reluctant to give sensitive information if they know they are being taped
iii) Transcribing the tapes before analysis is time-consuming and tedious

Observation

Observation is one of the few options available for studying records, mechanical processes, small children and complex interactive processes. Data can be gathered as the event occurs. Observation includes a variety of monitoring situations that cover non-behavioural and behavioural activities. It is commonly used in studies related to behavioural science. It has to be systematically planned and controlled and subjected to checks and controls on validity and reliability, and also constructed to serve a formulated research purpose for it to serve as a scientific tool for data collection. Direct observation is a measuring instrument to measure such traits as self-control, cooperativeness, truthfulness and honesty. One observes without asking questions to correspondents.

The Observer-Participant Relationship

Interrogation presents a clear opportunity for interviewer bias. The problem is less pronounced with observation but is still real. The relationship between observer and participant may be viewed from three perspectives:

- ➢ Whether the observation is direct or indirect
- ➢ Whether the observer's presence is known or unknown to the participant
- ➢ What role the observer plays

Guidelines for the Qualification and Selection of Observers

> Concentration: Ability to function in a setting full of distractions
> Detail-oriented: Ability to remember details of an experience
> Unobtrusive: Ability to blend with the setting and not be distinctive
> Experience level: Ability to extract the most from an observation study

Advantages of Observation

Observation enables one to:

1. Secure information about people or activities that cannot be derived from experiment or surveys
2. Reduces obtrusiveness
3. Avoids participant filtering and forgetfulness
4. Secures environmental context information
5. Optimizes the naturalness of the research setting
6. The advantages of observation include:
7. The researcher is enabled to record natural behaviour
8. It records natural behaviour thus bias is reduced
9. Observation is not expensive
10. It allows collection of a wide range of information
11. It is ideal in studying non-verbal communication

Disadvantages
1. Observation lacks control of variables in a natural setting
2. There is difficulty in quantification because it is mostly descriptive
3. It lacks privacy and has limited study scope
4. Observation studies use a smaller sample than survey studies
5. Difficulty of waiting for long periods to capture the relevant phenomena
6. The expense of observer costs and equipment
7. Reliability of inferences from surface indicators
8. The problem of quantification and disproportionately large records

Observation Forms, Schedules or Checklists

The researcher must define the behaviours to be observed and then develop a detailed list of behaviours. During data collection, the researcher checks off each as it occurs. This permits the observer to spend time thinking about what is occurring rather than on how to record it and this enhances the accuracy of the study.

Conference

The conference technique is a face to face discussion of a topic of interest. Experts are brought together at a common site. The group brainstorms to generate as many ideas on the problem as possible. The experts then evaluate and rate the suggestions. The most popular responses are determined. Finally the group discusses the strengths and weaknesses of the top suggestions and ranks the final choices.

Case Study

This involves a careful and complete observation of a social unit, be it a family, institution or cultural group. It normally places emphasis on depth rather than breadth. A case study concentrates on the full analysis of a limited number of events or conditions and their inter-relations.

Focus Group Discussion

A focused group is an organized discussion session. A panel of people meets for a short duration to exchange ideas, feelings, and experiences on a specific topic. A trained facilitator, using group dynamics and principles, guides participants through the meeting. Focus group meetings enable a researcher to gain a lot of information in a relatively short period of time.

Telephone Surveys

This is a direct talk with the interviewees over the phone.

Mail Surveys

This is the sending of questionnaires through the post office.

Computer Direct Surveys

These are interviews in which the interviewees enter their own answers directly into a computer.

Email Surveys

Similarly to computer direct surveys, email survey can be done by sending the questionnaire via email.

Pilot Testing

This is conducted to detect weakness in design and instrumentation and to provide proxy data for selection of a probability sample. It should draw subjects from the target population and stimulate the procedures and protocols that are designated for data collection. Pre-testing may rely on colleagues, respondent surrogates, or actual respondents to refine a measuring instrument. Pre-testing may be repeated several times to refine questions, instruments or procedures.

Validity and Reliability

According to Cook and Campbell (1979) "validity is the best available approximation to the truth or falsity of a given inference, proposition or conclusion". A test is valid when it measures what it is supposed to measure. How valid a test is depends on its purpose, e.g. a ruler may be a valid measurement for length but it is not a valid measurement of volume. The validity of a questionnaire depends on its reliability. If the questionnaire is not reliable then it cannot be valid

Reliability is the consistency of measurement or the degree to which an instrument measures the same way each time it is used under the same conditions with the same subjects. An instrument is considered reliable if the score of a person on the same test, given twice, is similar. Reliability is not measured but estimated. The quality of a research study depends to a large extent on the accuracy of the data collection procedures. Reliability and validity measures the relevance and correctness of the data.

Without the agreement of independent observers able to replicate research procedures, or the ability to use research tools and procedures that yield consistent measurements, researchers would be unable to satisfactorily draw conclusions, formulate theories, or make claims about the generalize ability of their research. In addition to its important role in research, reliability is critical for many parts of our lives, including manufacturing, medicine and sports. Reliability is such an important concept that it has been defined in terms of its application to a wide range of activities.

Reliability is influenced by random error. Random error is deviation from a true measurement due to factors that have not effectively been addressed by the researcher. As random error increases, reliability decreases.

Causes of Random Error
   i) Inaccurate coding
   ii) Ambiguous instruction to the subjects
   iii) Interviewer's fatigue
   iv) Interviewee's fatigue
   v) Interviewer's bias

The Test-Retest Technique

This involves administering the same instruments twice to the same group of subjects, but after some time. Stability reliability (sometimes called test, re-test reliability) is the agreement of measuring instruments over time. To determine stability, a measure or test is repeated on the same subjects at a future date. Results are compared and correlated with the initial test to give a measure of stability.

An example of stability reliability would be the method of maintaining weights used by the Kenya Bureau of Standards. Platinum objects of fixed weight (one kilogram, half kilogram, etc.) are kept locked away. Once a year they are taken out and weighed, allowing scales to be reset so they are "weighing" accurately. Keeping track of how much the scales are off from year to year establishes stability reliability for these instruments. In this instance, the platinum weights themselves are assumed to have perfectly fixed stability reliability.

Disadvantages

i) Subjects may be sensitized by the first testing, hence will do better in the second test

ii) Difficulty in establishing a reasonable period between the two testing sessions

Equivalent Form

Equivalent reliability is the extent to which two items measure identical concepts at an identical level of difficulty. Equivalency reliability is determined by relating two sets of test scores to one another to highlight the degree of relationship or association. In quantitative studies and particularly in experimental studies, a correlation coefficient, statistically referred to as r, is used to show the strength of the correlation between a dependent variable (the subject under study), and one or more independent variable, which are manipulated to determine effects on the dependent variable. An important consideration is that equivalency reliability is concerned with correlational, not causal, relationships.

For example, a researcher studying university Bachelor of commerce students happened to notice that when some students were studying for finals, their holiday shopping began. Intrigued by this, the researcher attempted to observe how often, or to what degree, these two behaviours co-occurred throughout the academic year. The researcher used the results of the observations to assess the correlation between studying throughout the academic year and shopping for gifts. The researcher concluded there was poor equivalency reliability between the two actions. In other words, studying was not a reliable predictor of shopping for gifts.

Two instruments are used. Specific items in each form are different but they are designed to measure the same concept. They are the same in number, structure and level of difficulty e.g. TOEFL, GRE.

The advantage of this method is that it estimates the stability of the data as well as the equivalence of the items in the two forms. The disadvantage is the difficulty in constructing two tests, which measure the same concept (time and resources).

Internal Consistency Technique

Internal consistency is the extent to which tests or procedures assess the same characteristic, skill or quality. It is a measure of the precision between the observers or of the measuring instruments used in a study. This type of reliability often helps researchers interpret data and predict the value of scores and the limits of the relationship among variables. For example, a researcher designs a questionnaire to find out about college students' dissatisfaction with a particular textbook. Analysing the internal consistency of the survey items dealing with dissatisfaction will reveal the extent to which items on the questionnaire focus on the notion of dissatisfaction.

Interrater Reliability

Interrater reliability is the extent to which two or more individuals (coders or raters) agree. Interrater reliability addresses the consistency of the implementation of a rating system.

A test of interrater reliability would be the following scenario: Two or more researchers are observing a high school classroom. The class is discussing a movie that they have just viewed as a group. The researchers have a sliding rating scale (1 being most positive, 5 being most negative) with which they are rating the student's oral responses. Interrater reliability assesses the consistency of how the rating system is implemented. For example, if one researcher gives a "1" to a student response, while another researcher gives a "5," obviously the interrater reliability would be inconsistent.

Interrater reliability is dependent upon the ability of two or more individuals to be consistent. Training, education and monitoring skills can enhance interrater reliability.

Ways of Improving Reliability

i) Minimize external sources of variation
ii) Standardize conditions under which measurements occurs

iii) Improve investigator consistency by using only well trained, supervised and motivated persons to conduct the research
iv) Broaden the sample of measurement questions by adding similar questions to the data collection instrument or adding more observers or occasions to an observation study
v) Improve internal consistency of an instrument by excluding data from analysis drawn from measurement questions eliciting extreme responses

Validity

Validity refers to the degree to which a study accurately reflects or assesses the specific concept that the researcher is attempting to measure. It is the degree to which results obtained from the analysis of data actually represent the phenomenon under study. It is the accuracy and meaningfulness of inferences, which are based on the research results. It has to do with how accurately the data obtained in the study represents the variables of the study. If such data is a true reflection of the variables, then inferences based on such data will be accurate and meaningful. Validity is largely determined by the presence or absence of systematic error in the data, e.g. using a faulty scale to measure.

Types of Validity

1. Construct Validity

Construct validity seeks agreement between a theoretical concept and a specific measuring device or procedure. For example, a researcher inventing a new IQ test might spend a great deal of time attempting to "define" intelligence in order to reach an acceptable level of construct validity. Construct validity can be broken down into two sub-categories: convergent validity and discriminate validity. Convergent validity is the actual general agreement among ratings, gathered independently of one another, where measures should be theoretically related. Discriminate validity is the lack of a relationship among measures which theoretically should not be related.

To understand whether a piece of research has construct validity, three steps should be followed. First, the theoretical relationships must be specified. Second, the empirical relationships between the measures of the concepts must be examined. Third, the empirical evidence must be interpreted in terms of how it clarifies the construct validity of the particular measure being tested.

2. Content Validity

Content Validity is based on the extent to which a measurement reflects the specific intended domain of content. Content validity can be illustrated using the following examples: Researchers aim to study mathematical learning and create a survey to test for mathematical skill. If these researchers only tested for multiplication and then drew conclusions from that survey, their study would not show content validity because it excludes other mathematical functions. Although the establishment of content validity for placement-type exams seems relatively straight-forward, the process becomes more complex as it moves into the more abstract domain of socio-cultural studies. For example, a researcher needing to measure an attitude like self-esteem must decide what constitutes a relevant domain of content for that attitude. For socio-cultural studies, content validity forces the researchers to define the very domains they are attempting to study. The usual procedure in assessing the content validity of a measure is to use professional or experts in the particular field. The instrument is given to two groups of experts; one group is requested to assess what concept the instrument is trying to measure. The other group is asked to determine whether the set of items or checklist accurately represents the concept under study.

3. Criterion Related Validity

Criterion related validity, also referred to as instrumental validity, is used to demonstrate the accuracy of a measure or procedure by comparing it with another measure or procedure which has been demonstrated to be valid. For example, imagine a hands-on driving test has been shown to be an accurate test of driving skills. By comparing the scores on the written driving test with the scores from the hands-on driving test, the written test can be validated by using a criterion related strategy in which the hands-on driving test is compared to the written test.

4. Predictive validity

This refers to the degree to which obtained data predicts the future behaviour of subjects, e.g. B. Com graduates.

5. Concurrent validity

This refers to the degree to which data are able to predict the behaviour of subjects in the present and not in the future, e.g. psychiatry.

Internal and External Validity

Researchers should be concerned with both *external* and *internal* validity.

i) External validity refers to the extent to which the results of a study are generalizable or transferable. External validity is the degree to which research findings can be generalized to populations and environments outside the experimental setting. It has to do with representativeness of the sample with regard to the target population.

ii) Internal validity refers to (1) the rigor with which the study was conducted (e.g. the study's design, the care taken to conduct measurements, and decisions concerning what was and wasn't measured) and (2) the extent to which the designers of a study have taken into account alternative explanations for any causal relationships they explore. In studies that do not explore causal relationships, only the first of these definitions should be considered when assessing internal validity. Internal validity depends on the degree to which extraneous variables have been controlled for in the study. Internal and external validity are inversely related to each other.

Threats to Internal Validity

1. History – occurrence of events that influence experimental units during the course of the study
2. Maturation – the biological or psychological processes which occur among the subjects in a relatively short time and which influence research findings
3. Instrumentation
4. Pre-testing – solution – use equivalent form tests

5. Statistical regression
6. Attrition – subjects dropping out of the study before completion; leads to error, bias in the sample
7. Differential selection – occurs when subjects are systematically selected for a study –volunteers and non-volunteers – bias leads error
8. Selection – maturation interaction
9. Ambiguity – when correlation is taken for causation
10. Apprehension – when people are scared to respond to your study
11. Demoralization – when people get bored with your measurements
12. Diffusion – when people figure out your test and start mimicking symptoms

Threats to External Validity
1. Accessible target population
2. Control of extraneous variables
3. Pre-test treatment interaction
4. Explicit description of the sample
5. Multi-treatment interference

Review Questions
i) Define data collection and state the sources of data
ii) Asses the data collection methods
iii) Differentiate between validity and reliability

CHAPTER SEVEN
DATA ANALYSIS AND PRESENTATION

Data Analysis and Interpretation

Managers need information, not raw data. Researchers generate information by analysing data after its collection. Data analysis usually involves reducing accumulated data to a manageable size, developing summaries, looking for patterns, and applying statistical techniques. Scaled responses on questionnaires and experimental instruments often require the analyst to derive various functions, as well as to explore relationships among variables.

Further, researchers must interpret these findings in light of the client's research questions or determine if the results are consistent with their hypothesis and theories. Increasingly, managers are asking research specialists to make recommendation based on their interpretation of data.

Reporting the Results

Finally, it is necessary to prepare a report and transmit the findings and recommendation to the manager for the intended purpose of decision making. The researcher adjusts the style and organization of the report according to the target audience, the occasion, and the purpose of the research. Reports should be developed from the manager's or information user's perspective.

In the end, the manager's foremost concern is solving the management dilemma; thus the researcher must accurately assess the manager's needs throughout the research process and incorporate this understanding into the final product, the research report. The management decision maker occasionally shelves the research report without taking action. Inferior communication of results is a primary reason for this outcome. With this possibility in mind the research specialist should strive for insightful adaptation of the information to the client's needs and careful choice of words in crafting interpretations, conclusions and recommendations.

Occasionally, organizational and environmental forces beyond the researcher's control argue against the implementation of results.

At a minimum*, a research report should contain the following*:

i) An *Executive Summary* consisting of a synopsis of the problem, findings and recommendations

ii) An *Overview of the Research*: The problem's background, literature summary, methods and procedures, and conclusion *iii)* A Section on *Implementation Strategies* for the recommendations

iv) A *Technical Appendix* with all the materials necessary to replicate the report

Research Process Issues

Although it is desirable for research to be thoroughly grounded in management priorities, studies can wander off target or be less effective than they should be.

Favoured-technique Syndrome

Not all researchers are comfortable with experimental design. The availability of a technique is an important factor in determining how research will be done or whether a given study can be done. Persons knowledgeable about and skilled in some techniques but not in others are too often blinded by their special competencies.

Company Database Strip-Mining

The existence of a pool of information or a database can distract a manager, seemingly reducing the need for other research. Data mining is often the starting point in decision-based research but rarely will such activity answer all management questions related to a particular management dilemma.

Unresearchable Questions

Not all management questions are researchable; not all research questions are answerable. To be researchable, a question must be one for which observation can provide the answer. Many questions cannot be answered on the basis of information alone.

Ill-Defined Management Problem

Some categories of problems are so complex, value-laden, and bound by constraints that they prove to be intractable to traditional forms of analysis. These questions have characteristics that are virtually the opposite of those of well-defined problems.

Politically Motivated Research

It is important to remember that a manager's motivations for seeking research are not always obvious. Managers might express a genuine need for specific information on which to base a decision. This is the ideal scenario for quality research.

Presentation and Analysis of Data

The main aim of statistics is to simplify the complexity of the quantitative data and to make them easily intelligible. Diagrams and graphs help to understand the information easily and in a comprehensive way. Business data like sales, production, and price are frequently presented in the forms of diagrams or graphs.

Diagrams

Diagram representation is best suited to spatial services and split into different categories whenever a comparison of the same type of data at different places is to be made. diagrams will be the best way to do that.

Advantages of Diagrams

i) They save time and labour
ii) Facilitate comparison
iii) They give an effective impression
iv) Easy to memorise
v) It makes information contained in the data readily intelligent
vi) Attractive way of representing data

Limitations of Diagrams

i) They don't give accurate results but a rough idea
ii) Technical knowledge is needed to construct a diagram
iii) One cannot compare diagrams when the units used are different hence the phenomena is not the same
iv) Diagrams can be misused easily

Construction of a Diagram

Any diagram drawn should be neat and clean so that it can attract the mind of the reader. A good diagram should have a brief heading on the top and the scale should be indicated clearly. All symbols to be used should be explained clearly so that it does not cause confusion.

Types of Diagrams

1. One-dimensional diagram – bar grams
2. Two-dimensional diagrams – for example rectangle square and circles
3. Pictograms and maps

Visual Displays of Data

In addition to numerical summaries of location, spread and shape, visual displays can be used to provide a complete and accurate impression of distribution and variable relationships.

i) Frequency table arrays data from highest to lowest values with counts and percentages. They are most useful for inspecting the range of responses and their repeated occurrence

ii) Bar charts and pie charts are appropriate for relative comparisons of nominal data

iii) Histograms are optimally used with continuous variables where intervals group the responses

iv) Stem and leaf displays present actual data values using a histogram type device that allows inspection of spread and shape

v) Box plots use the five-number summary to convey a detailed picture of a distribution's main body, tails and outliers

vi) Control charts display sequential measurements of a process together with a centre line and control limits. The selection of a control chart depends on the level of data one is measuring. It helps managers focus on special causes of variation by revealing whether a system is under control and substantiating results from improvements

vii) The Pareto diagram is a bar chart whose percentages sum to 100 percent. The causes of the problem under investigation are sorted in decreasing importance with bar height descending from left to right. Its pictorial array reveals the highest concentration of quality improvement potential in the fewest number of remedies

Analysis of Data

Analysis of data means the computation of certain indices or measures along with searching for patterns of relationship that exist among the grouped data. Analysis, particularly in case of survey or experimental data, involves estimating the values of unknown parameter of a population and testing of hypothesis for drawing inferences. Once the data begins to flow in, attention turns to data analysis. If the project has been done correctly, the analysis planning is already done.

Data Preparation

This includes editing, coding and data entry. These activities ensure the accuracy of the data and their conversion from raw form to reduced and classified forms that are more appropriate for analysis.

Data Processing Operations

The data, after collection has to be processed and analysed in accordance with the outline laid down for the purpose at the time of developing the research plan. This is essential for a scientific study and for ensuring that we have all relevant data for making contemplated comparisons and analysis. Processing implies editing, coding, classification and tabulation of certain measures, along with searching for indicators of relationships that exist among data groups.

Editing

Editing of data is a process of examining the collected raw data (especially in surveys) to detect errors and omissions and to correct these when possible. Editing involves a careful scrutiny of the complete questionnaires and or schedules. It is done to ensure that the data are accurate, consistent with other facts gathered, uniformly entered, as complete as possible and have been well arranged to facilitate coding and tabulation.

Editing can be in a form of field editing, which consists in the review of the reporting forms by the investigator, completing what the latter has written in abbreviated and/or in illegible form at the time of recording the respondent's responses. Another form of editing is central editing, which should take place when all forms or schedules have been completed and returned to the office and all these forms should undergo editing by a single editor in a small study and by a team of editors in case of a large inquiry.

Editing detects errors and omissions, corrects them when possible and certifies that minimum data quality standards have been achieved. The editor's purpose is to guarantee that data are:

 i) Accurate
 ii) Consistent with intent of the question and other information in the survey
 iii) Uniformly entered
 iv) Complete
 v) Arranged to simplify coding and tabulation

Field Editing

In large projects, field editing review is a responsibility of the field supervisor. It should be done soon after the data have been gathered. During the stress of data collection, the researcher often uses ad hoc abbreviations and special symbols. Soon after the interview, experiment or observation, the investigator should review the reporting forms. It is difficult to complete what was abbreviated or written in shorthand or noted illegibly if the entry is not caught that day. When entry gaps are present from interviews, a call back should be made rather than guessing what the respondent 'probably would have said'. Self-interviewing has no place in quality research.

Central Editing

For a small study, the use of a single editor produces maximum consistency. In large studies, the tasks may be broken down so that each editor can deal with one entire section. This approach will not identify inconsistencies between answers in different sections. However, this problem can be handled by identifying points of possible inconsistency and having one editor check specifically for them.

Rules to guide editors in their work
i) Be familiar with instructions given to interviewers and coders
ii) Do not destroy, erase or make illegible the original entry by the interviewer; original entries should be crossed out with a single line to remain legible
iii) Make all entries on an instrument in some distinctive colour and in a standardized form
iv) Initial all answers changed or supplied
v) Place initials and date of editing on each instrument completed

Coding

This refers to the process of assigning numerical or other symbols to answers so that response can be put into a limited number of categories or classes. These classes should be appropriate to the research problem under consideration. They must also possess the characteristics of exhaustiveness and also that of mutual exclusivity, which means that a specific answer can be placed in one and only one cell in a given category set.

It is necessary for efficient analysis and through it the several replies may be reduced to a small number of classes which contain the critical information required for analysis.

Coding decisions should be taken at the design stage of the questionnaire.

The classifying of data into limited categories sacrifices some data detail but is necessary for efficient analysis. Coding helps the researcher to reduce several thousand replies to a few categories containing the critical information needed for analysis. In coding, categories are the partitioning of a set and categorization is the process of using rules to partition a body of data.

Coding Rules
The categories should be:
i) Appropriate to the research problem and purpose; categories must provide the best partitioning of data for testing hypotheses and showing relationships
ii) Exhaustive
iii) Mutually exclusive

Coding Closed Questions
The responses to closed questions include scaled items and others for which answers can be anticipated. When codes are established early in the research process, it is possible to pre-code the questionnaire. Pre-coding is particularly helpful for data entry because it makes the intermediate step of completing a coding sheet unnecessary. The data are

accessible directly from the questionnaire. A respondent, interviewer, field supervisor or researcher is able to assign an appropriate numerical response on the instrument by checking, circling or printing it in the proper coding location.

Coding Open-Ended Questions

Open-ended questions are always used where insufficient information or lack of a hypothesis prohibits preparing response categories in advance, where there is a need to measure sensitive or disapproved behaviour, discover salience or encourage natural modes of expressions. Content analysis is always used to analyse open-ended questions. Converse and Presser (1986) define content analysis as a research technique for the objective, systematic and quantitative description of the manifest content of a communication.

Classification

Most research studies result in a large volume of raw data which must be reduced into homogeneous groups to get meaningful relationships. This necessitates classification of data, that is, the process of arranging data in groups or classes on the basis of common characteristics. Data having common characteristics are placed in one class and in this way the entire data get divided into a number of groups or classes.

Two Types of Classification

i) Classification according to attributes: Data classified on the basis of common characteristics which can be descriptive (such as literacy, sex, honesty etc.) or numerical (such as weight, height, income etc.). Data obtained this way on the basis of certain attributes are known as statistics of attributes

ii) Classification according to class intervals: Data which can be measured through some statistical units like income, production, age, weight etc. come under this category. They are classified on the basis of class-intervals. For instance, persons whose income, say, are within Kshs. 10,000 to kshs 15,000 can form one group

Tabulation

When a mass of data has been assembled, it becomes necessary for the researcher to arrange the same in some kind of concise and logical order. Tabulation is the process of summarizing raw data and displaying the same in compact form (in the form of statistical tables) for further analysis.

Importance of Tabulation

   i) It conserves space and keeps explanatory and descriptive statements to a minimum
   ii) It facilitates the process of comparison
   iii) It facilitates the summation of items and detection of errors and omissions
   iv) It provides a basis for various statistical compositions.

Tabulation can be done by hand or by mechanical or electronic devices, depending on the size and type of study, cost, time pressure and availability of tabulating machines or computers.

"Don't Know" Replies

"Don't know" replies are evaluated in light of the question's nature and the respondent. While many don't knows are legitimate, some result from questions that are ambiguous or from an interviewing situation that is not motivating. It is better to report don't knows as a separate category unless there are compelling reasons to treat them otherwise.

Data Entry

Data entry converts information gathered by secondary or primary methods into a medium for viewing and manipulation. Data entry is accomplished by keyboard entry from pre-coded instruments, optical scanning, real time keyboarding, telephone pad data entry, bar codes, voice recognition, optical mark recognition (OMR) and data transfers from electronic notebooks and laptop computers. Database programs, spreadsheets and editors in statistical software programs, e.g. SPSS and SAS, offer flexibility for entering, manipulating and transferring data for analysis, warehousing and mining.

Graphical Presentation

A graph is a pictorial presentation of the relationship between variables. The relationship between two quantities can be shown by the help of a graph, and use of graphs is a goodform of presentation, especially when working on large numbers of items.

The data are plotted on a graph as a series of points and these points are joined by the help of a line or curve.

Characteristics of a Graph

i) Must give a correct impression
ii) The graphs must have a clear and comprehensive title
iii) A good graph must not be overcrowded with curves
iv) The curve must be distinct
v) The scale on y and x axis must be suitable according to the given data

vi) A good graph must be neat and clean

Types of Graphs

Important types of graphs are:
   i) Time series graphs or Histogram
   ii) Z-charts
   iii) Scattergraphs
   iv) Semi-logarithmic graph or ratio scale graphs
   v) Lorenz curve
   vi) Graphs of frequency distribution

Time Series Graphs

In a time series, values of a variable are given at different periods of time. When such a graph is drawn, it demonstrates changes in the value of a variable with the passage of time. The graphical presentation of such a series is called a histogram.

The main aim of drawing such graphs is to have comparison to study:
   i) Changes in one variable over a period of time
   ii) Changes of two or more variable over a period of time

Examples of a time series include:
   i) Population of a country over a specific period of time

ii) Sales of a business enterprise over a period of time

iii) Price of some specific commodities over a period of time

iv) Temperature over a period of time

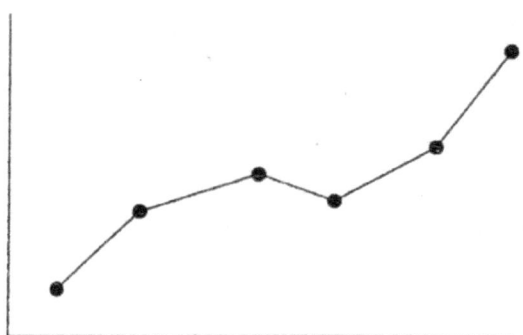

Z charts

A Z chart is simply a time series chart incorporating three curves for:
  i) Individual monthly figures
  ii) Monthly cumulative figure for the year
  iii) A moving annual total

The Z chart takes its name from the fact that the three curves lend to look like the letter Z.

Example of a Z-chart

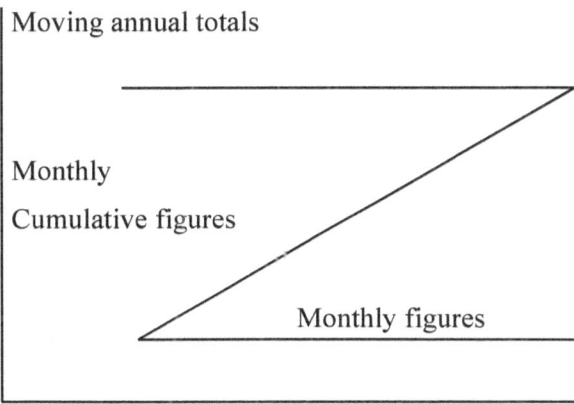

Scatter Graph

Scatter graphs are those graphs which are used to indicate the relationship between two variables. The x and y axes are used to represent variables. For this purpose, a line of best fit is established from the scatter graphs; this line indicates the relation or association between two variables.

This line may have a rising or falling trend, which shows positive and negative relationships between two variables respectively. For example, the sales and advertising expenditure of a company, whereby the y-axis represents sales and x axis represent advertising expenditure.

Example of a scatter graph

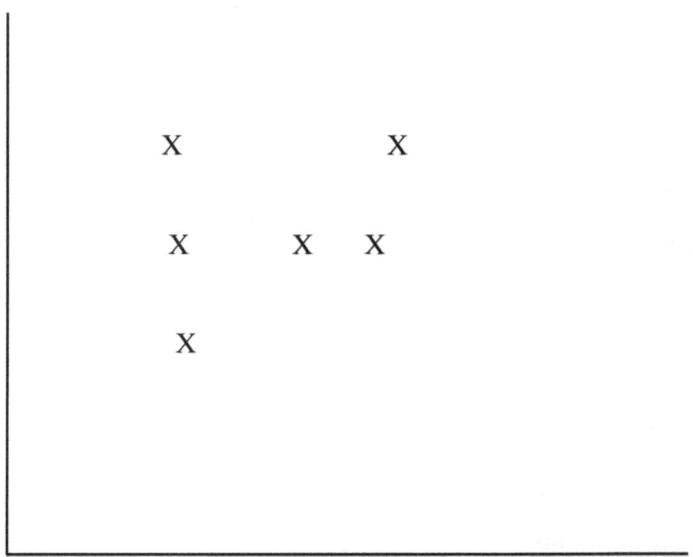

Semi-Logarithmic Graphs

A semi-logarithmic graph is that graph on which the vertical scale is logarithmic. It is also known as a scale graph. These graphs are important in studying relative movements, rather than absolute movements.

Semi-Logarithmic Graphs are generally used when:

i. Visual comparisons are to be made between series of greatly different magnitude
ii. The series are equated in non-comparable units
iii. The data are to be examined to see whether they are characterized by a constant rate of change

Lorenz Curve

This Lorenz curve measures dispersion. It was devised by Dr. Lorenz to measure inequalities of health distribution. It is used to measure the extent to which income is unevenly distributed between various income groups. The disparity of proportion is a common economic phenomenon. This disparity can be demonstrated by the help of Lorenz curve. A Lorenz curve is constructed as follows:

i) Write down the values of the two variable being plotted
ii) Express the variable or percentages of the total
iii) Compute the cumulative percentage of each variable
iv) Draw a horizontal and vertical axis and plot 0% to 100% on each axis
v) Mark the cumulative percentage on the graph and join the points
vi) Draw the line of an equal distribution by joining 0% to the 100% point by a straight line

Graphs of Frequency Distribution

The graphs of frequency distribution of continuous type are:

a) Ogive curve
b) Histogram
c) Frequency polygon
d) Frequency curve

1. **Ogive Curve**

This is obtained when the cumulative frequencies of a distribution are graphed. It is also called a cumulative frequency curve.

2. **Histogram**

This is a graph that represents the class frequencies in a frequency distribution by vertical rectangles. It consists of a series of rectangles having a base, measured along the x axis, proportional to the class interval, and an area proportional to the frequency.

MEASUREMENT

Introduction

While people measure things casually in daily life, research measurement is more precise and controlled. In measurement, one settles for measuring properties of the objects rather than the objects themselves. An event is measured in terms of its duration, i.e. what happened during it, who was involved, where it occurred etc. Measurement is the basis for all systematic inquiry because it provides us with the tools for recording differences in the outcome of variable change.

Definition of Measurement

Measurement is the procedure by which we assign numerals, numbers, or other distinguishing values to variables according to rules. These rules help us determine the kinds of values we will assign to certain observable phenomena or variables. They also determine the quality of measurement. Precision and exactness in measurement are vitally important. The measures are what are actually used to test the hypotheses. A researcher needs good measures for both independent and dependent variables.

Measurement is a three-part process that includes:
 i. Selecting observable empirical events
 ii. Developing a set of mapping rules: a scheme for assigning numbers or symbols to represent aspects of the event being measured
 iii. Applying the mapping rules to each observation of that event

Mapping rules have four characteristics:

1. Classification: Numbers are used to group or sort responses. No order exists

2. Order: Numbers are ordered. One number is greater than, less than or equal to another number

3. Distance: Differences between numbers are ordered. The difference between-any pair of numbers is greater than, less than or equal to the difference between any other pair of numbers

4. Origin: The number series has a unique origin indicated by the number zero.

This is an absolute and meaningful zero point

Measurement consists of two basic processes called conceptualization and operationalization, then an advanced process called determining the levels of measurement, and then even more advanced methods of measuring reliability and validity.

Conceptualization is the process of taking a construct or concept and refining it by giving it a conceptual or theoretical definition. Ordinary dictionary definitions will not do. Instead, the researcher takes keywords in their research question or hypothesis and finds a clear and consistent definition that is agreed upon by others in the scientific community. Conceptualization is often guided by the theoretical framework, perspective, or approach the researcher is committed to.

Operationalization is the process of taking a conceptual definition and making it more precise by linking it to one or more specific, concrete indicators or operational definitions. These are usually things with numbers in them that reflect empirical or observable reality. For example, if the type of crime one has chosen to study is theft (as representative of crime in general), creating an operational definition for it means at least choosing between petty theft and grand theft (false taking of less or more than $150).

Levels of Measurement

A level of measurement is a scale by which a variable is measured. For 50 years, with few detractors, science has used the Stevens (1951) typology of measurement levels (scales). There are three things to remember about this typology:

1. Anything that can be measured falls into one of the four types
2. The higher the level of measurement, the more precision in measurement
3. Every level up contains all the properties of the previous level

The four levels of measurement, from lowest to highest, are:

1. **Nominal level**. The observations are classified under a common characteristic, e.g. sex, race, marital status, employment status, language, religion etc. – helps in sampling
2. **Ordinal level**: items or subjects are not only grouped into categories, but they are ranked into

some order, e.g. greater than, less than, superior, happier than, poorer, above etc. – helps in developing a like scale

3. **Interval level**: numerals are assigned to each measure and ranked. The intervals between numerals are equal. The numerals used represent meaningful quantities but the zero point is not meaningful, e.g. test scores, temperature

4. **Ratio level**: Has all the characteristics of the other levels and in addition the zero point is meaningful. Mathematical operations can be applied to yield meaningful values, e.g. height, weight, distance, age, area etc.

Sources of Measurement Differences

The ideal study should be designed and controlled for precise and unambiguous measurement of the variables. Since 100% control is unattainable, error occurs. Much potential error is systematic (results from a bias) while the remainder is random (occurs erratically). Some of the major sources of error are:

1. **The respondent**: opinion differences that affect measurement come from relatively stable characteristics of the respondent, e.g. employee status, ethnic group and social class. Temporary factors like fatigue, boredom, anxiety and other

distractions also limit the ability to respond accurately and fully. Hunger, impatience or general variations in mood will also have an impact

2. **The situational factors:** any condition that places a strain on the interview or measurement session can have serious effects on the interviewer-respondent rapport. If another person is present, that person can distort responses by joining in, by distracting or by merely being present. If the respondents believe anonymity is not ensured, they may be reluctant to express certain feelings

3. **The measurer:** the interviewer can distort responses by re-wording, paraphrasing, or re-ordering questions. Stereotypes in appearance and action introduce bias. Inflections of voice or unconscious prompting with smiles and nods may encourage or discourage certain replies. Incorrect coding, careless tabulation and faulty statistical calculation may introduce further errors in data analysis

4. **The data collection instrument:** a defective instrument can cause distortion in two major ways:
    i. It can be too confusing and ambiguous, e.g. the use of complex words, leading questions, ambiguous meanings, multiple questions

ii. Leads to poor selection from the universe of content items. Seldom does the instrument explore all the potentially important issues

Measure of Central Tendency

Measure of central tendency (or statistical average) tells us the point about which items have a tendency to cluster. Such a measure is considered as the most representative figure for the entire mass of data. Measuring of central tendency is known as statistical average. Mean, median and mode are the most popular averages. Mean, also known as arithmetic average, is the most common measure of central tendency and may be defined as the value which we get by dividing the total of values of various given items in a series by the total number of items.

Qualities of a Good Average

i) It should be rigidly defined
ii) It should be based on all values
iii) It should be easily understood and calculated
iv) It should be least affected by the fluctuations of sampling
v) It should be capable of further algebraic or statistical treated

vi) It should be least affected by extreme values

Mean

Where x = the symbol for mean £X = Summation of observation value n = number of observation n = total number of items

The Median

This is the value of the middle item of service when it arranged in ascending or descending order of magnitude; it divides the series into two halves. The median is the middle score for a set of data that has been arranged in order of magnitude. The median is less affected by outlets and skewed data. In order to calculate the median, suppose we have the data below.

| 65 | 55 | 89 | 56 | 35 | 14 | 56 | 55 | 37 | 45 | 92 |

We first need to rearrange that data in order of magnitude (smallest first).

| 14 | 35 | 55 | 55 | 56 | 56 | 65 | 87 | 98 | 92 | 92 |

Our median mark is the middle mark, in this case 56.

Mode

The mode is the most frequent score in our data set. On a histogram it represents the highest bar in a bar chart or histogram. It is the most commonly or frequently occurring value in a series. The mode in a distribution is that item around which there is maximum concentration, hence it is the size of the item which has the maximum frequency.

Measure of Dispersion

This is the extent of scatter of items around a measure of central tendency. The degree to which numerical data tend to spread about an average value is called the variation or dispersion of the data. A measure of dispersion indicates the extent to which the individual observations differ, on average, from the mean or from any other measurer of central tendency.

Significance of Measuring Dispersion

   i) To determine the reliability of an average
   ii) To serve as a basis for the central of the variability
   iii) To compare two or more series with regard to their variability
   iv) To facilitate the use of the statistical measures

Properties of a Good Measurer of Dispersion

   i) It should be simple to understand
   ii) It should be rigidly defined
   iii) It should be easy to compute

iv) It should be based on each and every item of the distribution

Methods of Measuring Dispersion

The main methods of measuring dispersion are:

i) Range
ii) Quartile deviation or inter-quartile range
iii) Mean Deviation or average Deviation
iv) Standard Derivation
v) Lorenz curve

Range

The range is simply a measure of dispersion, i.e. between the highest or biggest value of a variable and the lowest or smallest one respectively. When dealing with a continuous variable the range can only be found accurately from the original data. Its value can only be estimated from a grouped frequency distribution; because of its simplicity, it is use in quality control work.

The Quartile Deviation

Quartiles are values of the variable that make up 25%, 50% or 75% of the population all the way through the distribution. There are three quartiles, the first is Ql, the second is Q2 and the third is Q3. The second quartile is the median, i.e. the variable that belongs to the item half-way through the distribution.

Mean Deviation

Mean deviation measures how far on average the readings are from the arithmetic mean. The median is very occasionally used instead of the arithmetic mean. If the data have a small spread about the mean, the mean deviation has a lower value than for data which show large variations about the mean.

To Calculate the Mean Deviation

i) Find the arithmetic mean X of the data
ii) Find the deviation of each reading from X
iii) Find the arithmetic mean of the deviations, ignoring their signs; i.e. the visits made to the local dispensary by members is as follows:

8, 6, 5, 5, 7, 4, 5, 9, 7, 4 Arithmetic mean = 60/6=10

Standard Deviation

Standard deviation is the most important measure of dispersion. It takes values of every observation into account but does not suffer from the same arithmetical deficiencies as the mean deviation.

$$\text{Variance} = \frac{\sum (x - x)^2}{n}$$

i) To calculate standard deviation for ungrouped data we use the formula:
ii) Find the arithmetic mean X of the data

iii) Find the deviation of each reading from X
iv) Square each of the variations
v) Total the squared deviation
vi) Divide this sum by the total number of reading to obtain the variance
vii) Find the square root of the variance to obtain the standard deviation

$$\text{Standard deviation} = \sqrt{\frac{\sum (x-x)}{n}}$$

Measure of Relationship

In statistics, dependence refers to any statistical relationship between two random variables or two sets of data.

Regression

This is the linear relationship between two or more variables. It is more widely used in statistical work than correlation. In regression analysis we are interested in "functional" relationship of variables, i.e. which the independent variable is and which the dependent variable is. Note that we can use the independent variables to predict or estimate the value of the dependent variables. Regression analysis is a term that refers to the use of observations/values of variables to calculate a curve of best fit so that we can make estimates and predictions about the behaviour of variables. The calculated line of best fit is called the regression line. The simplest method of calculating a regression line is by the three points method, which involves calculating the arithmetic mean.

Example

Advertising expenditure (x)	Sales Shs (y)
800	23000
1000	22000
1100	25000
1200	25000
1500	27000
1500	30000
1700	27000
1800	26000
1900	29000
2000	32000

All values of X and y (see figs above)

$$\overline{X} = \frac{\sum x}{N} = \frac{Sh. 14,500}{10} = sh.1,450$$

Least Squares Method

A better and more exact method of finding the line of best fit is to use the least squares method. This gives an algebraic equation connecting x and y. The type of equation that gives a straight line relationship between x and y is in this form.

Y = a + bx

Where: y is the value of the dependent variable

X is the value of the independent variable (a) and (b) are constants

Correlation

This is the linear relationship between two or more variables. The main interest is to find the degree and direction of this relationship. Correlation can be positive or negative depending on how the degree of correlation is calculated. Karl Pearson's coefficient of correlation is denoted by the symbol "v'. It is one of the very few symbols that are used universally for describing the degree' of correlation between two series.

The formula is:-

V =covariance of x and y

(Standard deviation of x) X (standard deviation of y)

$$V = \frac{\sum xy}{N \text{ xx } 6y}$$

Where

$X = x - x$ and $y = y - y$

$6x$ = standard deviation of series x

$6y$ = standard deviation of series y

N = number of pairs of observation

R = the "product movement" corrective coefficient

Correlation

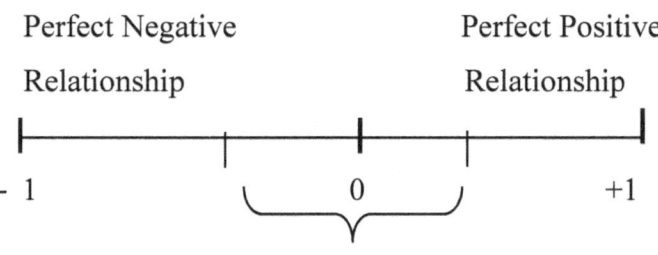

Weak relationship

Review Questions

i) Explain the process of reporting results

ii) Asses the various methods of data presentation

iii) Briefly explain what you understand by the following terms

    a) Measure of central tendency

    b) Measure of dispersion

    c) Range

    d) Quartile deviation

    e) Mean deviation

    f) Standard deviation

    g) Measure of relationship

    h) Regression

    i) Correlation

CHAPTER EIGHT
HYPOTHESIS TESTING

Basic Concept of Hypothesis Testing

Hypothesis testing is a statistical inferential procedure in which a statement based on some experimental or observational study is formulated, tested and then put through a decision process. Hypothesis is a researcher's anticipated explanation or opinion regarding the result of the study. A hypothesis states possible differences, relationships or causes between two variables or concepts. Hypotheses are derived from or based on existing theories, previous research, personal observations or experiences.

For example, in a study on productivity of labour within manufacturing industries, a researcher may hypothesize that more monetary incentives would lead to increases in productivity of labour or that provision of recreational facilities would raise productivity.

Formulating Hypotheses

A hypothesis is a researcher's prediction regarding the outcome of the study. It states possible differences, relationships or causes between two variables or concepts. Hypotheses are derived from or based on existing theories, previous research, personal observations or experiences.

The test of a hypothesis involves collection and analysis of data that may either support or fail to support the hypothesis. If the results fail to support a stated hypothesis, it does not mean that the study has failed; but it implies that the existing theories or principles need to be revised or retested under various situations.

Purpose of hypothesis
i) It provides direction by bridging the gap between the problem and the evidence needed for its solution
ii) It ensures collection of the evidence necessary to answer the question posed in the statement of the problem
iii) It enables the investigator to assess the information he or she has collected from the standpoint of both relevance and organisation
iv) It sensitizes the investigator to certain aspects of the situation that are relevant regarding the problem at hand
v) It permits the researcher to understand the problem with greater clarity and use the data to find solutions to problems
vi) It guides the collection of data and provides the structure for their meaningful interpretation in relation to the problem under investigation

vii) It forms the framework for the ultimate conclusions as solutions

Characteristics of a good hypothesis

A sound review of literature or of existing theories often leads to a good hypothesis.

1. Should state clearly and briefly the expected relationships between variables
2. Must be based on a sound rationale derived from theory or previous research or professional experience
3. Must be consistent with common sense or generally accepted truths
4. Must be testable
5. Must be related to empirical phenomena. Words like ought, should, bad should be avoided since they reflect moral judgment
6. Should be testable within a reasonable time
7. Variables stated in the hypothesis must be consistent with the purpose statement, objectives and operationalized variables in the method section
8. Must be as simple and as concise as the complexity of the concepts involved allows
9. It must be stated in such a way that its implications can be deduced in the form of empirical operations

with respect to which relationships can be validated or refuted

Assumptions and Limitations

i) An assumption is any fact that a researcher takes to be true without actually verifying it. It puts a boundary around the study and provides the reader with vital information, which influences the way results of the study are interpreted

ii) A limitation is an aspect of research that may influence the results negatively but over which the researcher has no control. A common limitation in social science studies is the scope of the study, which sometimes may not allow generalizations. Sample size may also be another limitation

Experiment of Studies or Hypothesis Testing

This are studies where the researcher tests the hypothesis of causal relationship between variables. Such studies reduce bias and increase reliability and also permit drawing inferences about causality. This is a form of research resign in which the major emphasis is on determining cause and effect relationships. Its main purpose is to understand which variables are the cause (independent variable) and which ones are the effects (dependent variable) of a phenomenon.

It also determines the nature of the relationship between the causal variables and the effects to be predicted.

Steps in Hypothesis Testing

i) A study can have one hypothesis or, where the study includes several variables, multiple hypotheses can be formulated

ii) Each hypothesis will usually express a predicted relationship between two or more variables or concepts

iii) Some authors have recommended that hypotheses which do not have strong support from theory/previous research or professional experience should be avoided

iv) Researchers usually find it difficult to formulate hypotheses in an area of knowledge that has very little previous research. In such an area not much is known that can support a hypothesis. They also find it difficult to formulate hypothesis in certain types of research. For example, where the research is exploratory, researchers usually omit the hypotheses and the study is guided by the stated objectives

v) It is very important for a researcher to give a lot of thought to his or her hypotheses because the whole study revolves around the stated hypotheses. It is the hypotheses that are put to empirical tests in a study

vi) The test of a hypothesis involves collection and analysis of data that may either support or fail to support the hypothesis. It is important to emphasize that testing a hypothesis does not "prove" or "disapprove" the hypothesis

vii) The collected data is then analysed to determine whether the hypothesized relationships exist. If the results fail to support a stated hypothesis, it does not mean that the study has failed. Such a situation actually implies that existing theories or principles need to be revised or tested under various situations

Types and Levels of Significance

Researchers recognize three types of hypotheses:;

i) Null hypotheses
ii) Alternative non-directional hypotheses
iii) Alternative directional hypotheses

Null Hypothesis

A null hypothesis is sometimes referred to as a statistical hypothesis. A null hypothesis always states that no real relationship or difference exists; any relationship between two variables or difference between groups is merely due to chance or error.

Example

There is no difference in the performance of national examinations between standard eight students from rural primary schools and standard eight students from urban primary schools in Kenya.

We can test the above hypothesis by sampling several schools from each region and working out an average score on the national examination for each region. We can then start by stating that the two averages will not differ, i.e. the null hypothesis states that the population mean of children in rural primary schools is equal to the population mean of children in urban schools.

Alternative Non-Directional Hypotheses

An alternative non-directional hypothesis is also referred to as a research hypothesis. This type of hypothesis states that there is a relationship or differences but the researcher does not know the nature of such a difference or relationship. An alternative non-directional hypothesis is suitable where previous research findings are conflicting or where a strong rationale to support a predicted relationship does not exist. Stating a hypothesis in a non-directional form is a conservative approach; the researcher avoids commitment to a specific outcome.

Examples

i) High alcohol content in the blood affects reaction time among truck drivers in Kenya. This hypothesis states that a relationship exists between the variables but the researcher does not indicate the direction of that relationship, i.e. does alcohol reduce or increase reaction time?

ii) There is a difference in the performance of national examinations between children from rural primary schools and children from urban primary schools. This hypothesis states that a difference between the two groups exists, but we are not told which group performs better than the other

Alternative Directional Hypothesis

An alternative directional hypothesis specifies the nature of the relationship or difference between variables. This means that a relationship may be stated as being greater than, less than, increased, decreased, higher than, lower than etc.

Where the researcher is not sure of the form of the relationship, he or she should not use a directional hypothesis, especially where there is a chance of obtaining an opposite relationship form the one hypothesized.

Example

1. High alcohol content in the blood decreases reaction time of truck drivers in Kenya

From previous studies and experiences it is highly likely that this hypothesis is borne out by the results of a research study. Even from common sense or general observation, drunk drivers take a longer time to react to dangerous situations compared to sober drivers.

"T"-test

A t-test is a special case of the analysis of variance (ANOVA). It is used to test whether there are significant differences between two means derived from two samples or groups at a specified probability level. For example, a researcher might want to compare IQ performance from rural and urban children. The researcher gets a sample of 30 subjects from a rural school and another 30 subjects from an urban school and administers the IQ test to both. A t-test is then used to compare the mean scores obtained by these two groups.

There are two types of tests;

The t-Test for Independent Samples

Independent samples are samples that are randomly formed, that is formed without matching. In such samples the members of one group are not related to the members of the other group in any systematic way other than that they are selected from the same population. It is assumed that the two groups are the same on the measure of interest at the beginning of the study. If they are different at the end of the study, then the treatment administered to the groups made them different. To determine whether there is a significant difference between the means of the two independent samples, a t-test is used.

The t-Test for non-Independent Samples

Non-independent samples refer to samples or groups that are formed by some type of matching. For example, if the same group is pre-tested on some dependent variable and then post-tested at a later date, the samples are non-independent and scores on the dependent variable are expected to be correlated. A special t-test for correlation or non-independent samples must be used to determine whether there is a significant difference between the means of the two samples or between the means for one sample at two different times.

A researcher may wish to compare groups on many variables. In this case, each comparison requires a separate t-test. To determine if the t value is significant, the researcher must decide on the significant level to use.

"F"-Test

An F-test is any statistical test in which the test statistic has an F-distribution under the null hypothesis. It is most often used when comparing statistical models that have been fit to a data set, in order to identify the model that best fits the population from which the data were sampled. Exact F-tests mainly arise when the models have been fit to the data using least squares. The name was coined by George. W. Snedecor, in honour of Sir Ronald A. Fisher. Fisher initially developed the statistic as the variance ratio in the 1920s.

Examples of F-Tests Include;

i) The hypothesis that the means of several normally distributed populations, all having the same standard deviation, is equal. This is perhaps the best known F-test and plays an important role in the analysis of variance (ANOVA)

ii) The hypothesis that a proposed regression model fits the data well

iii) The hypothesis that a data set in a regression analysis follows the simpler of two proposed linear models that are nested within each other

iv) Scheffe's method for multiple comparisons adjustments in linear models

Chi-Square Test

The chi-squared test is essentially *always a one-sided test*. Here is a loose way to think about it: the chi-squared test is basically a 'goodness of fit' test. Sometimes it is explicitly referred to as such, but even when it's not, it is still often in essence a goodness of fit. For example, the chi-squared test of independence on a 2 x 2 frequency table is (sort of) a test of goodness of fit of the first row (column) to the distribution specified by the second row (column), and vice versa, simultaneously. Thus, when the realized chi-squared value is way out on the right tail of its distribution, it indicates a poor fit, and if it is far enough, relative to some pre-specified threshold, we might conclude that it is so poor that we don't believe the data are from that reference distribution.

If we were to use the chi-squared test as a two-sided test, we would also be worried if the statistic were too far into the *left* side of the chi-squared distribution. This would mean that we are worried the fit might be *too good*. This is simply not something we are typically worried about. (As a historical side-note, this is related to the controversy of whether Mendel fudged his data. The idea was that his data were too good to be true.)

Chi-square is a statistical test commonly used to compare observed data with data we would expect to obtain according to a specific hypothesis. For example, if, according to Mendel's laws, you expected 10 of 20 offspring from a cross to be male and the actual observed number was 8 males, then you might want to know about the "goodness of fit" between the observed and expected. Were the deviations (differences between observed and expected) the result of chance, or were they due to other factors? How much deviation can occur before you, the investigator, must conclude that something other than chance is at work, causing the observed to differ from the expected? The chi-square test is always testing what scientists call the *null hypothesis*, which states that there is no significant difference between the expected and observed result.

Background

The Student's t-test and Analysis of Variance are used to analyse measurement data which, in theory, are continuously variable. But in some types of experiment we wish to record how many individuals fall into a particular category, such as blue eyes or brown eyes, motile or non-motile cells, etc. These counts, or enumeration data, are discontinuous (1, 2, 3 etc.) and must be treated differently from continuous data. Often the appropriate test is chi-squared (χ^2), which we use to test whether the number of individuals in different categories fits a null hypothesis (an expectation of some sort).

Chi-squared analysis is simple, and valuable for all sorts of things, not just Mendelian crosses. Here we build from the simplest examples to more complex ones. When you have gone through the examples you should consult the checklist of procedures and potential pitfalls.

Chi-square requires that you use numerical values, not percentages or ratios.

Step-by-Step Procedure for Testing Your Hypothesis and Calculating Chi-Square

i) State the hypothesis being tested and the predicted results. Gather the data by conducting the proper experiment (or, if working genetics problems, use the data provided in the problem)

ii) Determine the expected numbers for each observational class. Remember to use numbers, not percentages

iii) Calculate using the formula. Complete all calculations to three significant digits. Round off your answer to two significant digits

iv) Use the chi-square distribution table to determine significance of the value

a) Determine degrees of freedom and locate the value in the appropriate column

b) Locate the value closest to your calculated ^{2} on that degrees of freedom *df* row

c) Move up the column to determine the p value
v) State your conclusion in terms of your hypothesis
   a. If the p value for the calculated ^{2} is $p > 0.05$, accept your hypothesis. The deviation is small enough that chance alone accounts for it. A p value of 0.6, for example, means that there is a 60% probability that any deviation from expected is due to chance only. This is within the range of acceptable deviation
   b. If the p value for the calculated ^{2} is $p < 0.05$, reject your hypothesis, and conclude that some factor other than chance is operating for the deviation to be so great. For example, a p value of 0.01 means that there is only a 1% chance that this deviation is due to chance alone. Therefore, other factors must be involved

Computerised Data Analysis and Processing

Data Analysis

Data Analysis, it is the domain from which the data are harvested in a science or an engineering field. Data processing and information systems are considered terms that are too broad and the more specialized term data analysis is typically used. This is a focus on the highly-specialized and highly-accurate algorithmic derivations and statistical calculations that are less often observed in the typical general business environment. In these contexts data analysis packages like DAP, greti or PSPP are often used. This divergence of culture is exhibited in the typical numerical representations used in data processing versus numerical; data processing's measurements are typically represented by integers or by fixed point or binary coded-coded decimal representations of numbers, whereas the majority of data analysis's measurements are often represented by floating-point representation of rational numbers.

Computerized Data Analysis

Software packages are available for the analysis of quantitative and qualitative data. Each packed has different features and the researcher needs to choose carefully. The aim of all of the packages is to assist in the categorization and matching process. The packages can save time, but there is still a great deal of time required to set them up and input the data and check through the process.

Computer data processing is any process that a computer program does to enter data and summarize, analyse or otherwise convert data into usable information. The process may be automated and run on a computer. It involves recording, analysing, sorting, summarising, calculating, disseminating and storing data. Because data are most useful when well-presented and actually informative, data-processing systems are often referred to as information systems. Nevertheless, the terms are roughly synonymous, performing similar conversions; data-processing systems typically manipulate raw data into information, and likewise information systems typically take raw data as input to produce information as output.

Data processing may or may not be distinguished from data conversion, when the process is merely to convert data to another format, and does not involve any data manipulation.

Scientific data processing

Scientific data processing usually involves a great deal of computation (arithmetic and comparison operations) upon a relatively small amount of input data, resulting in a small volume of output. In the early days of computers, the emphasis was upon scientific data processing. This refers to a class of programs that organize and manipulate data, usually large amounts of numeric data. Accounting programs are the prototypical examples of data processing applications. In contrast, word processors, which manipulate text rather than numbers, are not usually referred to as data processing applications.

Processing

Basically, data are nothing but facts (organized or unorganized) which can be converted into other forms to make it useful, clear and practically used. This process of converting facts to information is called processing. Practically all naturally occurring processes can be viewed as examples of data processing systems where "observable" information in the form of pressure, light, etc. are converted by human observers into electrical signals in the nervous system as the senses we recognize as touch, sound, and vision. Even the interaction of non-living systems may be viewed in this way as rudimentary information processing systems. Conventional usage of the terms *data processing* and *information system*s restricts their use to refer to the algorithmic derivations, logical deductions, and statistical calculations that recur perennially in general business environments, rather than in the more expansive sense of all conversions of real-world measurements into real-world information in, say, an organic biological system or even a scientific or engineering system.

Commercial Data Processing

Commercial data processing involves a large volume of input data, relatively few computational operations, and a large volume of output.

Elements of Data Processing

In order to be processed by a computer, data needs first be converted into a machine readable format. Once data are in digital format, various procedures can be applied on the data to get useful information. Data processing may involve various processes.

Processing of data requires advance planning at the stage of planning the research design. This advance planning may convey such aspects as categorization of variables and preparation of dummy tables. This should be done with reference to the requirements of testing hypotheses/investigative questions. This type of preplanning ensures better identification of data needs and their adequate coverage in the tools for collection of data. Data processing consists of a number of closely related operations, viz.

i) Editing
ii) Classification and coding
iii) Transcription
iv) Tabulation

Editing

The first step in processing of data is editing of complete schedules/questionnaires. Editing is a process of checking to detect and or correct errors and omissions. Editing is done at two stages: first at the fieldwork stage and second at office.

i) Field Editing
ii) Office Editing

All completed schedules/questionnaires should be thoroughly checked in the office for Completeness, accuracy and Uniformity.

Classification and Coding

Coding

Coding means assigning numerals or other symbols to the categories or responses. For each question a coding scheme is designed on the basis of the con med categories. The coding schemes with their assigned symbols together with specific coding instructions may be assembled in a book. The codebook will identify a specific item of variable/observation and the code number assigned to each category of that item.

Categorization and Classification

The edited data are classified and coded. The responses are classified into meaningful categories so as to bring out essential patterns. By this method, several hundred responses are reduced to five or six appropriate categories containing critical information needed for analysis.

Editing and Classification

Classification can be done at any phase prior to the tabulation. Certain items like sex, age, type of house, and the like are structured and pre classified in the data collection form itself. The responses to open-ended questions are classified at the processing stage.

Categorization Rules

A classification system should meet certain requirements or be guided by certain rules. First, classification should be linked to the theory and the aim of the particular study. Second, the scheme should be exhaustive. That is, there must be a category for every response. Third, the categories must also be mutually exclusive, so that each case is classified only once.

Categorization and coding

How many categories should a scheme include? It is preferable to include many categories rather than a few, since reducing the number later is easier than splitting an already classified group of responses. However, the number of categories is limited by the number of cases and the anticipated statistical analysis.

Transcription

When only a few schedules are processed and hand-tabulated, tabulation can directly be made from the schedules. On the other hand, direct tabulation from the edited schedules/ questionnaires is difficult if the number of the schedules and the number of responses in them are large. Suppose an interview schedule contains 180 responses requiring tabulation and 210 simple and cross tables are to be constructed; each schedule has to be handled at least 210 times for tabulation. This will result in mutilation of the schedule, and omissions and commissions may easily occur in tabulation. In order to avoid these drawbacks, data contained in schedules/questionnaires are transferred to another material for the purpose of tabulation. This intermediary process is called 'transcription'.

Importance of Computerised Data

  i) Information empower
  ii) Accessibility to information
  iii) Edify, coding/tabulation
  iv) Information presentation

v) Storage elective storage

Advantages of Electronic Storage
i) It is extensible
ii) It is easy to distribute
iii) It is easy to interchange option
iv) It has low volume

Computers Assist Researchers in the Following Areas
1. **Knowledge Identification**

   This refers to checking the availability of knowledge. Knowledge identification may be fostered through borrowing different research works

2. **Access to Comprehensive Data**

   Computer circuit research is locating information and knowledge resources; in addition they provide free access to various and knowledge of the enhance knowledge use

3. **Knowledge Generation**

   Most computer programs can be used to generate new knowledge. They may support the elaboration of existing knowledge

4. **Knowledge Evaluation**

   Computer use enables a researcher to compare various ideas from different sources. Researchers may also compare their ideas with expert knowledge on the same data

5. **Knowledge Representation**

   Computer based tools provide functions for representations of knowledge. When graphs or tables are used for representations of individual knowledge they function as cognitive tools to augment the capital of human memory

6. **Knowledge Maintenance**

   This refers to the need for people using the World Wide Web for resource based learning or problem solving

7. **Data Storage**

   In order to cope effectively with the growing amount of the capacity of knowledge and knowledge resources in many domains there is a need for effective organisation of information

8. Computers also help in the collection of structured data items

Data Processing Operations

1. *Recording* – refers to the transfer of data into some form or document. It relates to the documentation of intermediate figures and facts resulting from calculations

2. *Verifying* – refers to the careful checking of the recorded data for any errors
3. *Duplicating* – refers to the reproduction of the data into many forms or documents
4. *Classifying* – refers to identifying and arranging items with like characteristics into groups or classes
5. *Sorting* – refers to arranging or rearranging data in a predetermined sequence to facilitate processing. Sorting is done in alphabetic or a numeric order
6. *Calculating* – refers to arithmetic manipulation of the data
7. *Summarizing and Reporting* – it is here where a collection of data is condensed and certain conclusions from the data are represented in a meaningful format that is clear, concise and effective
8. *Merging* – this operation takes two or more sets of data, all sets having been sorted by the same key, and puts them together to form a single sorted set of data
9. *Storing* – refers to placing similar data into files for future reference
10. *Retrieving* – refers to recovering stored data and/or information when needed

11. *Feedback* – refers to the comparison of the output(s) and the goal set in advance; any discrepancy is analysed, corrected, and fed back to proper stage in the processing operation

Review Questions
   i) Explain the basic concept of hypotheses testing
   ii) Explain the steps used in hypothesis testing
   iii) Asses the levels of significance
   iv) Discuss the T-test, F-test and the Chi-Square tests
   v) Asses the importance of computerized data

CHAPTER NINE
REPORT WRITING

Guidelines for Writing a Good Research Report

1. Break large units of text into smaller units, with headings to show organisation of the topics
2. Relieve difficult text with visual aids when possible
3. Emphasize important material and de-emphasize secondary material through sentence construction and judicious use of italicising, underlining, capitalizing and parentheses
4. Use ample space and wide margins to create a positive psychological effect on the reader
5. Choose words carefully, opting for the known and short rather than the unknown and long
6. Repeat and summarize critical and difficult ideas so readers can have time to absorb them
7. Review the writing to ensure the tone is appropriate
8. Proof read the final document to correct any errors
9. Use short paragraphs
10. Indent parts of text that represent listings, long quotations or examples
11. Use headings and subheadings to divide the report and its major sections into homogeneous topical parts

Report Writing Techniques

A quality presentation of research findings can have an inordinate effect on a reader's or a listener's perceptions of a study's quality. Recognition of this fact should prompt a researcher to make a special effort to communicate skilfully and clearly. Research reports contain findings, analysis, interpretations, conclusions and recommendations. Research reports differ depending on their aims and their readership. Reports should be clearly organized, physically inviting and easy to read. Writers can achieve these goals if they are careful with mechanical details, writing style and comprehensibility.

Research Report Format

The research format may differ slightly among institutions but there is a high degree of consensus on the format. In some institutions the conceptual framework is in chapter one while in others it is in chapter two. Other institutions have references as chapter six while other don't have chapter six. A typical research report format will have the following.

Preliminary Pages

The preliminary pages are usually numbered in roman numbers but the title page is not given any number

1. Cover Page/Title Page – contains the title/topic of research, name of student, sponsor and year
2. Declaration – This is the declaration by the student, supervisor and sponsor
3. Dedication – Dedication should be brief and usually limited to the family
4. Acknowledgements – Acknowledge all those that made your research possible in one or two paragraphs
5. Abstract – This is a summary of your report and it should include
    a) General objective
    b) Specific objectives
    c) Research design
    d) Target population
    e) Sampling technique
    f) Sample size
    g) Data collection methods
    h) Data analysis methods
    i) Findings
    j) Recommendations
6. Table of Contents
7. List of Tables
8. List of Figures
9. Abbreviations/Acronyms
10. Definition of Terms

CHAPTER ONE – INTRODUCTION TO THE STUDY

1.1 Introduction

This section tells the reader what to expect in that chapter and should be very brief, e.g. background of the study, statement of the problem, research objectives, research questions, significance of the study, limitations of the study and scope of the study.

1.2 Background of the Study

This section introduces us to the study in relation to the title. Introduction to background should give an insight into global trends narrowing/cascading down to local trends. This should be about two pages. In the background we include the profile of the study as 1.2.1

1.3 Statement of the Problem

A problem is a felt need, a question thrown forward for a solution, a deviation from what is known and what is desired to be known. A research problem refers to an issue or concern that puzzles the researcher. It is a concern that may result in the formulation of research questions. A research problem can also be viewed as an opportunity.

1.4 Objectives of the Study

1.4.1 General Objective

This is usually the same as the title, e.g. the main objective of this study was to determine the factors influencing the supply of Oil in Kenya with reference National oil Cooperation of Kenya.

1.4.2 Specific Objectives

These are based on variables chosen from the problem. The specific objectives must be SMART e.g.:

i) To ascertain the effects of infrastructure on the supply of oil in Kenya
ii) To determine the effects of foreign exchange on the supply of oil in Kenya
iii) To establish the effects of governance on the supply of oil in Kenya
iv) To identify the extent to which refinery capacity affects the supply of oil in Kenya

1.5 Research Questions

Research questions are questions that the researcher asks such that if answered then the research problem will be answered. They are usually open questions e.g.:

i) To what extent does infrastructure affect the supply of oil in K
ii) What is the effect of foreign exchange on the supply of oil in K
iii) How does governance affect the supply of oil in Kenya?
iv) To what extent does refinery capacity affect the supply of oil in Kenya?

1.6 Significance/Importance of the Study

Here we need to know who is going to benefit from your study, e.g. the organization, other researchers, the Government of Kenya etc.

1.7 Limitations of the Study

State the factors that hindered you from achieving your goals and how you overcame them, e.g. Non Cooperation, Bureaucracy, Confidentiality, etc.

1.8 Scope of the Study

This is the scope in terms of content scope, geographical scope and time scope

CHAPTER TWO – LITERATURE REVIEW

2.1 Introduction

Explain to the readers what to expect in the chapter

2.2 Review of Theoretical Literature

This covers literature by other authors based on your variables. Only the variable in the title and objectives should be discussed. Each variable should be discussed in about 3 – 4 pages from different authors. Literature review should be done in continuous prose and every paragraph must have a source

2.3 Critical Review

Tell us what other authors have said, what you think they have not said and how you will fill the gap left by the authors. Do not criticize but only critique. Depending on the report, this can be limited to a paragraph for each variable; e.g.:

> According to Agboola (2001) use of ICT has influenced the content and quality of banking operations. He argues that ICT presents great potential for business process

reengineering of Banks. Investment in information and communication technology should form an important component in the overall strategy of banking operators to ensure effective performance. It is imperative for bank management to intensify investment in ICT products to facilitate speed, convenience, and accurate services, or otherwise lose out to their competitors. Whereas this is true, the author does not tell us how competition affects the use of ICT in the banking sector. This study therefore intends to find out how competition affects the use of ICT in the banking sector in Kenya.

2.4 Summary

Here we have a summary of any literature that you feel is important from the 3-4 pages of your literature review. Cover all the variables precisely, in a paragraph for each variable

2.5 Conceptual Framework

A conceptual framework is defined as "a set of broad ideas and principles taken from relevant fields of enquiry and used to structure a subsequent presentation" (Reichel and Ramney, 1987). It explains either graphically or in narrative form the main dimensions being studied, or the presumed relationships among them. It is a framework showing the relationship between the independent variables and the dependant variable e.g.:

Figure 2.6 Conceptual Framework

Independent Variables **Dependent Variable**

Efficiency

Cost

Security

Use of ICT in the Banking Sector

Competition

Customer Satisfaction

Source: Author (2013)

Since this is your own conceptualization the relationship between the independent variables and the dependant variable must be interpreted.

CHAPTER THREE – RESEARCH DESIGN AND METHODOLOGY

3.1 Introduction

Introduce to the readers what to expect in the chapter

3.2 Research Design

Indicate the research design to be used and support it with a relevant authority who has justified the use of that design. The design must be suitable for your study

3.3 Target Population

Research population, according to Mugenda and Mugenda (2008) refers to entire group of individuals, events or objects having common characteristics or attributes. Babbie (1975)

defines population as the theoretically specified aggregation of survey elements. Target population is the complete unit of study interest. It is better understood by the use of a table, e.g.:

Table 3.1 Target Population

Category of Staff	Target Population	Percentage
Senior Managers	6	11
Supervisors	15	28
Technicians	33	61
Total	**54**	**100**

Source: Author (2013)

3.4 Sampling Technique

Sampling technique is the process of selecting a number of individuals or objects from a population such that the selected group contains element representative of the characteristics found in the entire group (Orotho 2002). Sometimes when the population is too large a sample can be used. If the population is small a census can be used. The technique of sampling should be based on your research and support it with a relevant authority who justifies its use. A table can be used, e.g.:

Table 3.2 Sample Size

Category of Staff	Target Population	Sample Size	Percentage
Senior Managers	6	5	11
Supervisors	15	12	28
Technicians	33	26	61
Total	**54**	**43**	**100**

3.5 Data Collection Methods

Here indicate the methods/instruments used for data collection, justifying the use of each method. Support the use by citing relevant authorities. Also include the pre-testing/piloting (validity and reliability) of the data collection instrument. One should also indicate how they will administer the questionnaire

3.6 Data Analysis Methods

Indicate the methods used to analyse your data. This will largely depend on the instrument used for data collection. Also indicate how data will be presented and justify both analysis and presentation methods

CHAPTER FOUR – DATA ANALYSIS, PRESENTATION AND INTERPRETATION

4.1 Introduction

Introduce what the chapter contains

4.2 Presentation of Findings

Quantitative data is analysed in form of tables and presented in figures (pie charts, graphs, etc.) and the interpretation is done. All questions asked in the questionnaire must be analysed

4.3 Summary of Data Analysis

The qualitative data is analysed in narrative form

CHAPTER FIVE - SUMMARY OF FINDINGS, CONCLUSIONS AND RECOMMENDATIONS

5.1 Introduction

Introduce what is to be expected in the chapter

5.2 Answers to Research Questions

State the research questions as they are in chapter one (1.5) and answer them using the extent or rating questions

5.3 Conclusions

Conclude as per the variables, preferably a paragraph for each

5.4 Recommendations

Recommend on each variable based on your findings

5.5 Suggestion for Further Studies

It is assumed that your research is not conclusive. Even from your limitations and scope it may show that you did not cover all the areas necessary to make your research conclusive. This necessitates that you suggest areas where other researchers can do research to supplement your research

Dissemination of Research Findings

The length, style and content is very important in dissemination of a report. The target group has to be considered when preparing a report. All the interested parties should get the report. The cost of dissemination must also be considered. Ensure that there is free access of information both on the research being conducted and on the findings of the research.

Review Questions
   i) Asses the process of preparing a research report
   ii) Explain the process of disseminating a research report

CHAPTER TEN
ISSUES IN RESEARCH

Ethics in Research

Ethics are norms or standards of behaviour that guide moral choices about our behaviour and our relationship with others. Ethics differ from legal constraints, in which generally accepted standards have defined penalties that are universally enforced. The goal of ethics in research is to ensure that no one is harmed or suffers adverse consequences from research activities. Research involves the voluntary participation and trust of your participants. It is your ethical responsibility as a researcher to treat your subjects with dignity and avoid violating this trust.

As the research is designed, several ethical considerations must be balanced, e.g.

i) Protect the rights of the participant or subject
ii) Ensure the sponsor receives ethically conducted and reported research
iii) Follow ethical standards when designing research
iv) Protect the safety of the researcher and team
v) Ensure the research team follows the design

Ethical Considerations in Research

1. Right to Privacy

Protect the privacy of the respondents who agree to provide you with data for your research. Do not disclose this information to any members of your staff who do not need to know it, and don't ever sell information gathered through research to other companies without the express permission of your participants. If you do need to reveal the identity of your research participants for any reason, let them know beforehand so they can provide informed consent.

All individuals have a right to privacy and researchers must respect that right. The privacy guarantee is important not only to retain validity of the research but also to protect respondents. Once the guarantee of confidentiality is given, protecting that confidentiality is essential. The researcher can protect respondent's confidentiality in several ways, which include:

i) Obtaining signed nondisclosure documents
ii) Restricting access to respondent identification
iii) Revealing respondent information only with written consent
iv) Restricting access to data instruments where the respondent is identified
v) Non-disclosure of data subsets

Researchers should restrict access to information that reveals names, telephone numbers, address or other identifying features. Only researchers who have signed non-disclosure, confidentiality forms should be allowed access to the data. Links between the data or database and the identifying information file should be weakened. Individual interview response sheets should be inaccessible to everyone except the editors and data entry personnel.

Occasionally, data collection instruments should be destroyed once the data are in a data file. Data files that make it easy to reconstruct the profiles or identification of individual respondents should be carefully controlled. For very small groups, data should not be made available because it is often easy to pinpoint a person within the group. Employee satisfaction survey feedback in small units can be easily used to identify an individual through descriptive statistics.

Privacy is more than confidentiality. A right to privacy means one has the right to refuse to be interviewed or to refuse to answer any question in an interview. Potential participants have a right to privacy in their own homes, including not admitting researchers and not answering telephones. They have the right to engage in private behaviour in private places without fear of observation.

To address these rights, ethical researchers can do the following:
  i) Inform respondents of their right to refuse to answer any questions or participate in the study
  ii) Obtain permission to interview respondents
  iii) Schedule field and phone interviews
  iv) Limit the time required for participation
  v) Restrict observation to public behaviour only

2. Clear Objectives

When conducting ethically sound research, your subjects should have a clear idea of your research intentions.

3. Informed Consent

Customers who participate in your research should know that they are doing so. It is unethical to film customers making purchasing choices and then review these films for clues about purchasing behaviour unless your customers know that you are filming them, and consent to the process. Although gathering this type of consent may change the data you receive because subjects may behave differently if they know they are being observed, failure to do so is a violation of their rights.

Securing informed consent from respondents is a matter of fully disclosing the procedures of the proposed survey or other research design before requesting permission to proceed with the study. There are exemptions that argue for a signed consent form. When dealing with children, it is wise to have a parent or other person with legal standing sign a consent form. If the researchers offer only limited protection of confidentiality, a signed form detailing the types of limits should be obtained. For most research, oral consent is sufficient.

In situations where respondents are intentionally or accidentally deceived, they should be debriefed once the research is complete. Debriefing involves several activities following the collection of data e.g.

i) Explanation of any deception
ii) Description of the hypothesis, goal or purpose of the study
iii) Post study sharing of results
iv) Post study follow-up medical or psychological attention

According to Neuman and Wiegand (2000), a full blown consent statement would contain the following:

1. A brief description of the purpose and procedure of the research, including the expected duration
2. A statement of any risks, discomforts or inconveniences associated with participation

3. A guarantee of anonymity or at least confidentiality, and an explanation of both
4. The identification, affiliation and sponsorship of the research as well as contact information
5. A statement that participation is completely voluntary and can be terminated at any time without penalty
6. A statement of any procedures that may be used
7. A statement of any benefits to the class of subjects involved
8. An offer to provide a free copy of a summary of the findings

4. Third-party Obligations

If you are conducting research as a third party, such as an independent consultant, it is your ethical obligation to provide honest, objective data based on carefully crafted questions. Phrase your survey in order to provide honest, accurate answers rather than trying to extract information as easily as possible. Choose a subject group that will provide the most useful, relevant information for the company that hired you, rather than simply working with a group because they are easy to interview.

5. Ethical Treatment of Participants

In general, the research must be designed in such a manner that the respondent does not suffer physical harm, discomfort, pain, embarrassment or loss to privacy. To safeguard against these, the researcher should follow the following guidelines:

i) Explain the study benefits
ii) Obtain informed consent
iii) Explain respondent's rights and protection

Whenever direct contact is made with a respondent, the researcher should discuss the study benefits, being careful to neither overstate nor understate the benefits. An interviewer should begin an introduction with his or her name, the name of the research organisation and a brief description of the purpose and benefits of the research. This puts the respondent at ease, lets them know to whom they are speaking and motivates them to answer questions truthfully. Inducements to participate, financial or otherwise, should not be disproportionate to the task or presented in a fashion that results in coercion.

Deception occurs when the respondents are told only part of the truth or when the truth is fully compromised. The benefits to be gained by deception should be balanced against the risks to the respondents. When possible, an experiment or interview should be designed to reduce reliance on deception. In addition, the respondent's rights and well-being must be adequately protected. In instances where deception in an experiment could produce anxiety, a subject's medical condition should be checked to ensure that no adverse physical harm follows.

6. Ethics and the Sponsor

There are ethical considerations to keep in mind when dealing with the research client or sponsor. Whether undertaking product, market, personnel, financial or other research, a sponsor has the right to receive ethically conducted research.

(a) Confidentiality

Sponsors have a right to several types of confidentiality, including sponsor non-disclosure, purpose non-disclosure and findings non-disclosure

i) Sponsor non-disclosure

Companies have a right to dissociate themselves from the sponsorship of a research project. Due to the sensitive nature of the management dilemma or the research question, sponsors may hire an outside consulting or research firm to complete research projects; this is often done when a company is testing a new product idea, to avoid potential consumers from being influenced by the company's current image or industry standing. If a company is contemplating entering a new market, it may not wish to reveal its plans to competitors. In such cases, it is the responsibility of the researcher to respect this desire and device a plan to safeguard the identity of the sponsor

ii) Purpose non-disclosure

This involves protecting the purpose of the study or its details. A research sponsor may be testing a new idea that is not yet patented and may not want the competitor to know his plans. It may be investigating employee complaints and may not want to spark union activity. The sponsor might also be contemplating a new public stock offering, where advance disclosure would spark the interest of authorities or cost the firm thousands of shillings

iii) Findings non-disclosure

If a sponsor feels no need to hide its identity or the study's purpose, most sponsors want research data and findings to be confidential, at least until the management decision is made

(b) Right To Quality Research

An important ethical consideration for the researcher and the sponsor is the sponsor's right to quality research. The right entails:

i) Providing a research design appropriate for the research question
ii) Maximizing the sponsor's value for the resources expended
iii) Providing data handling and reporting techniques appropriate for the data collected

From the proposal through the design to data analysis and the final report, the researcher guides the sponsor on the proper techniques and interpretations. Often sponsors would have heard about a sophisticated data handling technique and will want it used even when it is inappropriate for the problem at hand. The researcher should propose the design most suitable for the problem. The researcher should not propose activities designed to maximize researcher revenue or minimize researcher effort at the sponsor's expense. The ethical researcher should report findings in ways that minimize the drawing of false conclusions. He should also use charts, graphs and tables to show the data objectively, despite the sponsor's preferred outcomes.

7. Degree to Which the Research Questions Has Been Crystallized

Occasionally, research specialists may be asked by sponsors to participate in unethical behaviour. Compliance by the

researcher would be a breach of ethical standards. Some examples to be avoided are:
1. Violating respondent confidentiality
2. Changing data or creating false data to meet a desired objective
3. Changing data presentations or interpretations
4. Interpreting data from a biased perspective
5. Omitting sections of data analysis and conclusions
6. Making recommendations beyond the scope of the data collected

The ethical course often requires confronting the sponsor's demand and taking the following actions:
1. Educating the sponsor on the purpose of research
2. Explain the researcher's role in fact finding versus the sponsor's role in decision-making
3. Explain how distorting the truth or breaking faith with respondents leads to future problems
4. Failing moral suasion, terminate the relationship with the sponsor

8. Researchers and Team Members

Researchers have an ethical responsibility to their team's safety as well as their own and also protecting the anonymity of both the sponsor and the respondent

(a) Safety

It is the researcher's responsibility to design a project so the safety of all interviewers, surveyors, experimenters, or observers is protected. Several factors may be important to consider in ensuring a researcher's right to safety; e.g. some urban areas and undeveloped rural areas may be unsafe for research assistants, therefore a team member can accompany the researcher. It is unethical to require staff members to enter an environment where they feel physically threatened. Researchers who are insensitive to these concerns face both research and legal risks

(b) Ethical behaviour of assistants

Researchers should require ethical compliance from team members just as sponsors expect ethical behaviour from the researcher. Assistants are expected to carry out the sampling plan, to interview or observe respondents without bias and to accurately record all necessary data. Unethical behaviour, such as filling in an interview sheet without having asked the respondent the questions, cannot be tolerated. The behaviour of the assistants is under the direct control of the responsible researcher or field supervisor. If an assistant behaves improperly in an interview or shares a respondent's interview sheet with an unauthorized person, it is the researcher's responsibility. All researchers' assistants should be well trained and supervised

(c) Protection of anonymity

Researchers and assistants protect the confidentiality of the sponsor's information and the anonymity of the respondents. Each researcher handling data should be required to sign a confidentiality and nondisclosure statement

9. Unethical Practices

i) It is unethical to interview children without their parents' permission
ii) It is unethical to intelligently collect data for another company
iii) It is unethical to make recommendations beyond your study
iv) It is also unethical to publish the report if the source of the data says you shouldn't publish it

10. Plagiarism

Plagiarism is the presentation of someone else's ideas or words as your own. Whether deliberate or accidental, plagiarism is a serious and punishable offence in research. Students found guilty of plagiarism fail in research projects and may be disqualified from pursuing their career. Deliberate or accidental plagiarism occurs when a writer draw words, phrases or passages from other people's work and present them verbatim as their own work without providing complete documentation or source citation

Deliberate Plagiarism

i) Copying or downloading someone else's work and passing it off as your own without proper source citation

ii) Handing in as your work, a paper you have bought, had a friend write or copied from another student

iii) Summarizing or paraphrasing someone else's ideas without acknowledgement in a source citation

Accidental Plagiarism

i) Forgetting to put quotation marks around another writer's words

ii) Omitting a source citation for someone else's ideas without acknowledgement in a source citation

To avoid plagiarism the researcher should always acknowledge other people's ideas that are not common knowledge

Problems Encountered in Implementation of Research

1. Lack of scientific training in the methodology of research
2. Lack of competent researchers
3. Attitude towards research
4. Copying of data – Some researchers merely copy other international studies or studies which have

been done by researchers/students of other universities. This is a crime and should not be condoned

5. Manipulation of data – Every researcher tries or does one or the other kinds of manipulation of data. This never reveals the reality
6. Lack of availability or access to literature needed – This is a major problem faced during the literature review. The lack of availability of access to the Internet, ignorance of the way to search needed articles from journals and other databases are related problems
7. Lack of confidence to take up a new study, especially exploration studies. The fear of the result and fear of not able to answer questions during presentations
8. Unavailability of permission to do research
9. Some business establishments usually don't allow a third party inside to conduct research. This may be due to security reasons or may be due to lack of confidence in keeping the confidentiality of the data or names
10. Publishing research may be expensive
11. Once the study is completed, the next step will be publishing. Printing and binding may turn out to be expensive

Recommendations

i) Informed consent – Essentially, this means that prospective research participants must be fully informed about the procedures and risks involved in research and must give their consent to participate

ii) Guarantee confidentiality – They are assured that identifying information will not be made available to anyone who is not directly involved in the study.

iii) Training – Researchers should be trained in order to carry research in more competent way

iv) Provide the necessary literature

v) Provide the necessary funds

Reference List

In research the term "reference" applies to materials that have been referred to or quoted in the study. The reference list is usually at the end of the project report or paper. The reference list provides the information necessary to identify and retrieve each source. Researchers should choose references judiciously and must include only the sources that were used in the preparation of the research project.

References cited in the text must appear in the reference list. Conversely, each entry in the reference list must be cited in the text. The author must make sure that each source referenced appears in both places and that the text citation and reference list entry are identical.

Reference List Format and Order

i) The reference list format should provide the surname, initials, year of publication (in bracket), title, edition, publisher and place of publishing
ii) The list should be in alphabetical order
iii) Indent 2nd line
iv) Begin with books, then journals and magazines

Examples

Ateka, C. (2013), *Research Methodology and Design*, 1st Edition, Mount Kenya Publishers, Thika - Kenya

Kamau, J. & Onyango, T. (2007), *Referencing in Research*, 2nd Edtition, Longonot Publishers, Nairobi-Kenya

Mutiso, O.K. & Kiptoo S.C. (2002), *Understanding the Basics of Research*, 3rd Edition, Konza Publishers, Machakos-Kenya

Oresi, S.N., Onchoke S.N. & Ombuna, G.N. (2004), *Research Made Easy*, 1st Edition, Onchoke Publishers, Nairobi-Kenya

Vicky, O.K, Nyabuku, N.M. & Matundra, P.B. (2006), *The History of Research*, 5th Edition, Sakawa Publishers, Kisii-Kenya

Zaituni, X.M., (2012), *Choosing a Research Design*, 1st Edition, Mshenangu Publishers and Printers, Mombasa-Kenya

Review Questions

i) Explain the ethical issues considered in research
ii) Explain what you understand by plagiarism
iii) Discuss the factors that must be considered when making recommendations
iv) Asses the styles of referencing

REFERENCES

Alan Thomas (Editor) (2007): *Research Skills for Policy and Development: How to Find Out Fast*, Sage.

Bliss, O., Monk, M.M. and Ogborn (1983). *Questionnaire Construction and Question Writing for Research*, Sterling Press, Western Cape

Collis, J. (2004), *Business Research*, 2nd Edition, Palgrave Macmillan, London.

Cooper, D, R and Schindler P, M (2006), *Business Research Methods*, 9th Edition, McGraw-Hill International Edition, New Delhi.

Dr Andrew Sumner (2008): *International Development Studies: Theories and Methods in Research and Practice*, Sage.

Earl R. Babbie (2010): *The Basics of Social Research*, Wadsworth Publishing.

Jeremy Holland (Editor) (2005): Methods in Development Research: Combining Qualitative and Quantitative Approaches, *Practical Action*.

Jonathan, (2004), *The Foundation of Research*, Palgrave Macmillan, London

Kombo, D.K. and Tromp, D.L.A. (2006), *Proposal and Thesis Writing*, Paulines Publications Africa, Nairobi

Kothari, C.R. (1997). *Research methodology, Methods and Techniques*, 2nd edition

Mugenda, O.M. and Mugenda, A.G. (1999). *Research Methods: Quantitative and Qualitative Approaches*, Acts Press, Nairobi

Orodho, A.J. and Kombo, D.K. (2002). *Research Methods*, Kenyatta University, Institute of Open Learning, Nairobi

Patten, M.L. (2002). *Understanding Research Methods: An Overview of the Essentials,* 3rd Edition, Pyrczak Publishing, Los Angels

Philip, J.S. and Pugh, M.T. (1994). *Research Methodology: Methods and Techniques*, Light Publishers, New Delhi

Rita C. Richey (2007): *Design and Development Research: Methods, Strategies, and Issues*, Routledge.

Saunders, M., & Lewis, P. (2003). *Research methods for business students* (3rd Ed.). Harlow, England: Prentice Hall.

Sekaran.U, (2006), *Research Methods for Business: A Skilled Building Approach,* 4th Edition

Wisker, G. (2001), *The Post Graduate Research Handbook* , Palgrave Macmillan London

www.ingramcontent.com/pod-product-compliance
Lightning Source LLC
Chambersburg PA
CBHW031615210526
45464CB00004B/1584